Pastoral Care
with the Poor

Charles Kemp

Abingdon Press
Nashville and New York

PASTORAL CARE WITH THE POOR

Copyright © 1972 by Abingdon Press

All rights in this book are reserved. No part of the book may be reproduced in any manner whatsoever without written permission of the publishers except brief quotations embodied in critical articles or reviews. For information address Abingdon Press, Nashville, Tennessee.

Library of Congress Cataloging in Publication Data

KEMP, CHARLES F. 1912-   . Pastoral care with the poor. Bibliography: p.   . 1. Poor. 2. Church and the poor. 3. Pastoral theology. I. Title
BV639.P6K44   362.5   72-926

ISBN 0-687-30295-1

MANUFACTURED BY THE PARTHENON PRESS AT NASHVILLE, TENNESSEE, UNITED STATES OF AMERICA

Acknowledgments

Many people have contributed to the material found in these pages. The following have all shared in the development of the program or the evaluation of the manuscript at one level or another.

The participants in the original project conducted by the Pastoral Care and Training Center of Brite Divinity School, Texas Christian University, were as follows:

Theological students serving as pastoral counselors and community chaplains representing the Pastoral Care and Training Center.

John Cook
Ron Franklin
Russell Sanders
John Woodall
James Abel
Virginia Brittain
R. T. Bolerjack
Pastoral consultants:

The Rev. Elmer McBride, pastor of Christ Holy Sanctified Church, Fort Worth, Texas.

The Rev. Cornelius Stearns, pastor of Christian Methodist Episcopal Church, Fort Worth, Texas.

The Rev. Steve Larsen, pastor of Urban Ministries, Fort Worth, Texas.

The Rev. James Ellison, chaplain at John Peter Smith Hospital, Fort Worth, Texas.

Consultants in special fields:

Dr. Fernando Torgerson, dean, School of Social Work, University of Texas at Arlington, social work consultant.

Dr. Robert Glen, professor of psychiatry, Southwest Medical School, Dallas, Texas, psychiatric consultant.

Mr. Walter Steele, Jr., visiting associate professor of law, School of Law, Southern Methodist University, Dallas, Texas, legal consultant.

Dr. Marcus Bryant, professor of pastoral psychology, Brite Divinity School, Fort Worth, Texas, theological consultant.

Mr. John McDonald, executive secretary of the Alcohol Information Center, formerly counselor in the Poverty Program in Fort Worth, coordinator of activities and procedures.

Mr. Charles H. Sanders, director, Pastoral Care and Training Center, Fort Worth, Texas, treasurer.

Several colleagues who also were project directors or consultants with the total program of "The Ministry in the Seventies" conducted by the Stone Foundation and the National Council of Churches were kind enough to read the manuscript and made many helpful suggestions. We are indebted to them for their willingness to render assistance even though conducting projects of their own, or acting as consultants on all seventeen projects.

Dr. Wayne E. Oates, professor of psychology of Religion, Southern Baptist Seminary, Louisville, Kentucky, and a project director.

Dr. Granger Westberg, professor of pastoral theology, Hamma School of Theology, Wittenberg, Ohio, and a project director.

Dr. Speed Leas, Director of COMMIT, Los Angeles Urban Training Center, consultant to the total project.

Dr. E. Mansell Pattison, associate professor of psychiatry and human behavior, University of California, and consultant to the total project.

Dr. Daniel Day Williams, professor of theology, Union

Theological Seminary, New York, and consultant to the total project.

I also asked several friends and colleagues to read and evaluate the material. Each person was selected because he had had unique and extensive experience in one or all of the areas discussed. Each was asked to make suggestions from his own particular specialty and perspective.

Mr. Andy Perpener, director of emergency food and medical service, Community Action Agency, Fort Worth, Texas.

Mr. Barton Hunter, executive secretary, Department of Church and Society, United Christian Missionary Society, Indianapolis, Indiana.

The Rev. Paul Sims, pastor, Community Christian Church, Fort Worth, Texas.

Mr. William Hall, associate professor of missions, Brite Divinity School, Texas Christian University, Fort Worth, Texas.

Mr. Richard Hoehn, assistant professor of church in society, Brite Divinity School, Texas Christian University, Fort Worth, Texas.

Mr. Russell Sanders, who was my student assistant at the time of the project, and Mrs. Jane Brabb helped in the preparation of the bibliography.

In addition to these persons who helped with the project or evaluated the manuscript there were literally hundreds of individuals who are alluded to in the case studies. Our indebtedness to them all is more than can be expressed.

Mrs. Jane Brabb and Mrs. Dixie Deen typed the manuscript through several revisions.

Many of the thoughts of the persons mentioned above were incorporated into the material, and much of what is of value is due to their suggestions and criticisms. Responsibility for the final copy is my own.

I also want to express appreciation to H. Rhea Gray of the Stone Foundation and to Douglass Lewis of the National Council of Churches, who guided the total project and with whom it has been a pleasure to work.

Contents

Foreword

In recent years in this country a great deal of time and effort in the church has been spent on how one trains persons to be effective ministers. Seminaries are constantly revising their curricula while their students protest that the curricula are irrelevant. Pastors complain that they were inadequately trained for the ministry in which they find themselves. Laymen feel that pastors are not really ministering to their needs. In short, the issue of what an effective ministry is for our day and how to train persons for that ministry has been and remains a central and crucial issue for the church today.

It was out of that concern that the W. Clement and Jessie V. Stone Foundation originated and funded a project designed to explore and develop new models and methods of training persons for the pastoral ministry in the 1970s. Seventeen project directors and eight consultants from the fields of psychology, psychiatry, sociology, theology, and action training, along with the foundation staff, assembled in the summer of 1969 to explore the needs in our society which demand ministry and how to train persons to perform that ministry. Out of these consultations came seventeen experimental projects which were located in theological education centers from Boston to Los Angeles, Atlanta to Chicago. Each was original in its approach and the problem it was attacking, but all were designed to be exploratory, ground-breaking, and direction-giving.

Shortly after the project was under way, a major reorganization in the role and function of the Stone Foundation made it impossible for the foundation staff to give the project the kind of ongoing supervision and coordination that it required. A grant was made to the Department of Ministry of the National Council of Churches for the continuation and fulfillment of the project. Under its supervision all the projects were completed by the summer of 1971. The objectives, methods, and results of each project have been published in a book, *Exploration in Ministry,* which is available through the Stone Foundation.

The ideas, insights, and materials contained in this book are the result of one of these projects which was carried out by Dr. Charles Kemp and Dr. Marcus Bryant of the Department of Pastoral Care, Brite Divinity School, Texas Christian University. Their work is exemplary of the innovation sought in the Ministry in the Seventies Project. They dealt with one of the most nagging and difficult problems facing our society and focused their concern with real depth on how one ministers and trains persons to minister in that context. In so doing, they have made a significant contribution to the church's contemporary ministry and to those whose existence is plagued by poverty.

It was extremely gratifying to witness the dedication, persistence, and commitment which these men brought to the project. As with the other projects, all of which have something unique to contribute, the impact of this project reaches far beyond that which can be committed to writing. Its impact has already been felt in depth by those who worked in the project—the staff, pastors, and people in the poverty areas touched by the project.

Nevertheless, the readers who must necessarily be exposed to the experience secondhand and in writing will find this book extremely helpful in understanding the key issues for a ministry in poverty areas and can glean numerous practical insights and ideas which can facilitate a ministry in that area.

The directors of this project are to be commended for the contribution they have made to the preparation of persons for the church's ministry in the vital areas. It has been a great pleasure to work with them in this project and to learn and be stimulated by the work they have done.

G. Douglass Lewis
Project Coordinator
Ministry in the Seventies Project

Introduction: The Purpose and Design of This Study

This material was prepared as a result of a study on pastoral care and poverty conducted by the Department of Pastoral Care of Brite Divinity School, Texas Christian University. The study was made possible by a grant from the W. Clement and Jessie V. Stone Foundation of Chicago under the supervision of the Department of Ministry of the National Council of Churches.

The purpose is to state some of the basic principles that should govern pastoral care with the poor.

The entire study covered approximately a three-year period. It consisted of the utilization of a group of pastors working in a poverty area, several advanced theological students who were assigned responsibilities in the area, several persons who were fulfilling specialized ministries as chaplains in a county hospital, in Goodwill Industries, and in a street, or night, ministry. In addition special consultants were secured representing the fields of urban law, psychiatry, social work, and theology. A whole series of experimental pilot projects, seminars, evaluations, and reviews were conducted to evaluate the project.

Central to the study was an attempt to understand what

took place during actual ministry to persons in need—whether the need was personal, legal, physical, emotional, or spiritual. Literally hundreds of cases of actual situations were presented where a pastor or theological student had attempted to provide ministry to persons who lived in what would be considered poverty.

The findings have been condensed into as brief a form as possible. We have not attempted to include either statistical findings or extensive clinical material. Both are available, although the study was definitely more clinical than statistical.

The format is as follows. Each general principle is given a title and is summarized in a brief statement that is written in italics. A brief paragraph or two explains the statement. At the close of most paragraphs a brief example is given. Case studies would have been more valuable, but space did not permit any more than a thumbnail sketch as an illustration. It is hoped that these brief allusions to actual situations will add a note of reality to the material. It is easy to state a principle; it is difficult to apply it in actual experience. These sketches, brief as they are, keep reminding us of the complexity and reality of life situations.

Where it was possible we have included situations that illustrate the principle being discussed. Some could have been used as examples in several sections. Others are not as specifically descriptive of the previous material as we would like. Since over fifty different topics are discussed, inevitably this is true. We wanted to preserve the idea of discussing principles and thinking in terms of actual life situations whether the illustration fits exactly or not.

The illustrations came from many sources. Some from students, some from pastors, some from chaplains, some from consultants. In each case the word "pastor" has been used to describe the person serving as minister. The people represent many denominations and no denomination. They represent different races—white, black, and brown. Some are children, some elderly, some middle-aged. They have been selected from several hundred examples which were recorded on tape or in writing, any of which could have been used. No names have been used. The information provided is so brief and has been sufficiently altered so that no one can be indentified. In fact, most illustrations could describe many persons and are representative of thousands in cities throughout the country. They all have two things in common: (1) they all were poor, and (2) they all came to the attention of a pastor in one way or another.

We began this study to ask certain basic questions. How do people in a poverty area think of their pastors? Do they think of them in terms of pastoral care? Do they take their problems to them? And if so, what kind of problems do they take? Are there pastors who have been proven effective in the poverty area? What is the explanation of their effectiveness? Do the methods described in the books on pastoral care and taught in the seminaries apply in a poverty area? If not, what modifications need to be made? How does ministry in a poverty area differ from a ministry of pastoral care in a suburban area? How can training for pastoral care be improved?

We feel we have answers to some of these questions, partial answers to others, and need much more experience and investigation to answer them all. In no sense do we present our findings as final or complete. We hope they will be helpful, but more important, that they will stimulate others to seek more extensive answers to these same questions.

One of the chief problems in preparing this material was the limitation in space. We said things in sentences that needed paragraphs, and things in paragraphs that needed volumes. The material is meant to be only introductory in nature. Some may feel it is too simplistic. We trust the reader will make allowances. We hope the topics discussed will be suggestive enough to stimulate others to evaluate their experiences and perhaps interest a few to do more thorough investigation and research into this most important subject.

This manual is prepared with four groups in mind:

(1) Theological students who may be assigned to serve in a

14

poverty area either as a field work assignment or as a part of a clinical pastoral education program.

(2) Pastors of rural or suburban churches who occasionally are called upon to minister to someone from a poverty area, or who may have a few parishioners who are poor.

(3) Pastors of churches whose congregation includes a rather high percentage of people who live in a poverty area, but many who are middle- or upper-class.

(4) Pastors whose churches serve a constituency that is predominantly from a poverty area.

The first two groups need this kind of manual the most. The latter two groups are already familiar with these situations from personal experience, although the material that is discussed here may sharpen their observation and help them evaluate their own ministry, and thus become a bit more effective than they were. In the main, we were thinking of pastors and theological students who come from a middle-class background and need help in understanding how to work with the poor.

"Blessed is he who considers the poor." The Pastoral Care Center where this consideration took place.

I.   Backgrounds: Biblical and Historical

The Biblical Imperative

One who ministers to the poor fulfills a basic requirement of both the Old Testament and the New.

"Blessed is he who considers the poor!" (Psalm 41:1.) Throughout both the Old Testament and the New there are numerous admonitions to consider and care for the poor. These take two forms. One is a demand for justice, which includes a warning and strong condemnation of those who exploited the poor. The other is a call to service, an appeal to personal and practical concern. This concern was an integral part of the Old Testament law; it was central in the preaching of the prophets; it was at the heart of Jesus' message of love and compassion. The parable of the Good Samaritan implies that anyone who is facing misfortune or need is our neighbor and should be the subject of our concern. In the parable of the last judgment in the twenty-fifth chapter of Matthew, Jesus listed the righteous as those who fed the hungry, clothed the naked, visited the sick and imprisoned; and then he said, "As you did it to one of the least of these my brethren, you did it to me." (For a more extensive list of biblical passages, see Appendix A.)

Reverend G. was a pastor of a small congregation in what the sociological studies would call a "blighted" area of the city. Most of the people in the neighborhood of his church were on welfare; housing was substandard, infant mortality was high. The incidence of crime, disease, etc. was the highest in the city. Yet he stayed, although several opportunities for more prestigious, more lucrative positions were offered him. He ministered to the sick, the elderly, the children. He preached, called, counseled (in an untrained way), often gave advice, distributed food and clothing. Like John Frederic Oberlin, "he could not resist the cry of the needy." He felt his calling was to minister to the poor, and he did.

A Tradition of Compassion

One who works with the poor links himself with a historic tradition of Christian compassion.

Throughout the long history of the church there has always been kept alive the biblical spirit of compassion and concern. For generations the church was almost the only agency that demonstrated any extensive practical concern.

It found expression in such men as St. Francis of Assisi caring for the lepers and the poor, William Booth in the slums of London, John Wesley and his charitable activities that were coupled with his evangelistic efforts, Jane Addams in Chicago, Walter Rauschenbusch and his cry for reform.

It has resulted in the establishment of institutions such as

17

the Salvation Army, the Volunteers of America, and Goodwill Industries. It has been instrumental in creating agencies such as Hull House in Chicago, social settlements, home mission projects.

Many wonder about the place of the church today. They ask what has happened to the spirit of compassion and concern that motivated such men for so many generations. (See "Men of Compassion," Appendix B.)

The pastor of a church of some three hundred members, many of whom were poor, kept a record of his pastoral calls and interviews over a three-month period. Just a few of the situations listed were as follows: "Visited the home of Mr. and Mrs. J. D. Their problem—family conflict. Mrs. Y. came to office. Her husband is a heavy drinker. Set fire to the house. Woman, middle-aged, has night job which enables her to support her teen-age son; needs transportation to work. Family called at 2:30 A.M., daughter in hospital. Need funds for medical and hospital bills. Woman attended church. Wanted to talk afterward about family problem, possible divorce. Visited in hospital (as did regularly). Young woman concerned about twelve-year-old son and his religious training. Called in home of man about recurring head-aches; Dr. says no reason. Family asked to accompany them to court. Father being tried. Pastor went. Woman felt very guilty, trouble sleeping. Confessed something she had done. Family needs money for food. Loaned from church fund." These are but a few of the cases listed. There are those who still keep the spirit of compassion alive. "Inasmuch as you did it to one of the least of these. . . ."

God and the Ghetto

One who works in a poverty area must constantly reexamine his own theology and religious convictions so that they be adequate for the situation.

It is the Christian faith that God is alive, that God understands, that God forgives, that God redeems, that God empowers, that God sustains, that God suffers with his people.

It is the Christian faith that the church is, or should be, a redemptive fellowship, proclaiming a gospel of love and justice, challenging men to lives of service and faith. It is the Christian faith that man should live a life of service, that he should treat all men as brothers, that he should live a life of love.

The problem of poverty is so vast that some have suggested we need a theology of the ghetto, a theology of poverty. We do not need a theology of poverty any more than we need a theology of affluence or a theology of the suburbs. What we need is an awareness and an application of the theology we know—in the ghetto and the suburbs.

People in poverty need an awareness of God's presence and his care as much as they need new welfare laws. Pastors who work with the poor need a constant awareness of the reality of the Christian faith both to sustain their own spirits and to sustain the people they are trying to serve.

A Mexican-American family went through a period of great difficulty, illness, and financial reverses. One member of the family said, "Why is God punishing us?" The husband and father said, "God is not punishing us, God is with us." Later he said to his pastor it was his religious faith that sustained him in the time of crisis.

"We began this study to ask certain basic questions. . ."

II. The Contemporary Scene: The Culture of Poverty

What Is Meant by Poverty

One who would work with the poor must understand what is meant by poverty.

There are many definitions of poverty. The simplest procedure is to state the amount of income needed for an individual or for a family, as the case may be. Anything below that is considered poverty. The problem, of course, is that the amount needed fluctuates and varies with the family.

A simple definition is to ask the question, Does the need calculated according to family budget exceed the income? If so, there is poverty.

The Social Security Administration defines it this way: "If annual money income is less than three times the cost (in current prices) of a minimal diet for the persons in that household, it is poverty."

The Council of Economic Advisers includes another element when it says, "By poor we mean those who are not now maintaining a decent standard of living, those whose basic needs exceed their means to satisfy them."

John Kenneth Galbraith feels it is a relative matter. "People are poverty-stricken when their income level, even if adequate for survival, falls markedly behind that of the community. Then they cannot have what the larger community regards as the minimum necessary for decency, and they cannot wholly escape, therefore, the judgment of the larger community that they are indecent." (*The Affluent Society*, p. 75.)

One author carries the relative idea further. He speaks of the "psychologically poor" as those "who manage to eat enough to keep going but who suffer as keenly as those below them on the economic ladder because they have so little hope of ever enjoying what the rest of American society routinely enjoys." (*Paradox of Poverty in America*, p. 39.)

Perhaps the simplest definition is: to be poor means not having enough money to live decently. We are not interested in technical definitions. We are concerned if people's circumstances do not permit them to live respectably and with dignity.

A pastor who said 98 percent of his counseling was with the poor submitted this definition of poverty. Whether it is original or not we do not know.

"Poverty is loneliness, and no one cares; poverty is never getting a suit or dress you may want; poverty is Mom fixing spaghetti in every way known to man, so you won't guess you are eating it for the tenth time this week; poverty is being sick, waiting all day to see the doctor and being told he is out; poverty is seeing other kids with dads and wishing that you had one; poverty is being a bad boy at four-years-old; poverty is never being completely filled up at mealtime; poverty is badly fitting shoes so that your feet always hurt; poverty is having your landlord live so far away that he never fixes anything, and paying $50 a month for one room with no heat, no lights, and no running water; poverty is being a school drop-out at six; poverty is being picked up by police on suspicion of murder because you are on the wrong side of the street, or you are the wrong color, wear a trenchcoat and live on Railroad Avenue; poverty is being cold, alone, and frightened and having only $58 a month left after you have paid your rent, and when other bills are due; poverty is having babies and not wanting them; poverty is applying for a job and being turned down over and over because you have no skills, or don't know how to apply; poverty is being called a delinquent because you live in a public housing project; poverty is never owning anything you can call yours, not even a corner which is your own; poverty is also anger, fear, irresponsibility, lack of motivation, alcoholism, prostitution, despair, and loneliness; poverty is falling down and no one comes to kiss the dirt away."

The Culture of Poverty

One who would work with the poor must understand the nature of the culture of poverty and its impact on personality.

Michael Harrington, in his famous book *The Other America,* says definitely that there is a culture of poverty. In his words, "Poverty in the U.S. is a culture, an institution, a way of life. . . . Everything about them [the poor], from the condition of their teeth to the way in which they love, is suffused and permeated by the fact of their poverty." He contends that they "grow up in a culture that is radically different from the one that dominates society." (*The Other America,* pp. 23, 24.) As a result they have different attitudes toward the church, toward the law, toward the police, toward counseling, toward almost everything.

Harrington says poverty "twists and deforms the spirit." "The American poor are pessimistic and defeated and they are victimized by mental suffering to a degree unknown in suburbia." (*The Other America*, p. 10.)

Such feelings can affect one's entire future outlook. Dick Gregory said, "Poor is a state of mind you never grow out of, but being broke is just a temporary position." (*Nigger*, p. 25.) Continuous poverty during childhood leaves impressions that are never wholly lost.

The *Encyclopedia of Social Work* states that the poor are characterized by three things.

(1) Preoccupation with the present rather than the future.
(2) An assumption that impersonal forces control one's destiny.
(3) A cynical view of government.

A young couple with two children discussed their problem with a pastor. They have no church affiliation, but were willing to see a pastor at the suggestion of the police. Both work but seem unable to handle their money. They were married at 15 and 16 years of age. When they were hard up he pimped for her as a prostitute. Their relationship was strained; the children were not receiving any care. Attempts were made to combine counseling with the help of Family Service.

A family called their pastor at 2:30 A.M. The husband is 37, the wife 36, both work to care for eight children, ranging in age from 8 to 20. An 18-year-old daughter has been in the hospital and could not be released because of lack of money.

Status, Wealth, and Poverty

In America many things contribute to status: work, housing, income, education, organizations and groups to which one belongs. The poor have none of these.

John Kenneth Galbraith says there are three basic benefits from having money. They are: (1) satisfaction in the power which money provides, (2) the ability to secure and possess the things which money can buy, and (3) the status and recognition that our society gives the men of wealth. (*The Affluent Society*, p. 76.)

Money can be a means to many things: education, art, travel, medical care, housing, etc., all of which are denied to the poor.

R. is a 58-year-old black man who came seeking food. He had been injured in an industrial accident; his arm was in a cast. He had been unable to work for some time, in fact had difficulty carrying a bag of groceries. He did not have bus fare, so the pastor offered to take him home in his car. When he got in the car he began to cry. Somewhat apologetically he said he had "never cried like this before." He said he was crying both because he was grateful for people who would help and because his pride was hurt. He had always supported himself and his family and was embarrassed when he couldn't. Arriving at the shack where he lived he again expressed appreciation that "there are people who do care about us poor folks."

The Extent of the Problem

One who would work with the poor must be aware of the vast extent of the problem.

Statistics at best indicate trends. They give some idea of the immensity of the problem. Estimated percentages of poverty usually vary from 15 to 20 percent of the total population. As one author put it, eighty percent of America lives in comparative comfort, the rest are poor. Using these figures, the number of people that are poor would run well into the millions.

Statistics are in a constant state of change. Unemployment goes up and down as the economy changes. Statistics vary with the community. Some depressed areas, such as Appalachia, have a high incidence of poverty; in other areas it is lower, but no area escapes entirely. It is not just an urban crisis, though there are many urban poor. There are also many poor in rural areas. Some estimate from 8 to 11 million. A rural slum is not much better than an urban slum. Even suburbia must be included. Some poor live in the suburbs.

The two groups most affected are the very young and the very old. It is estimated that half of the poor are under twenty-one (12 million) and one third are over sixty-five. The young without adequate education are the last to be hired and the first to be laid off. This is also true of the elderly. Although many of the elderly do not wish to work, and some are unable to work, there are others who could, who need the income, who desire something to do. Yet like the young they often cannot find employment.

Although racial groups have particular problems, especially Indians, the blacks, and Latin Americans, the problem includes whites as well. Government figures indicate 69 percent of all people living in poverty are white.

These statistics, staggering as they are, do not tell the whole story. There are many more whom Harrington describes as living "just the other side of poverty." While they are not officially counted as "poor," they share all the concerns, frustrations, and feelings of the poor because they still exist at levels below that which is necessary for human decency.

The pastor is concerned about statistics only as they indicate trends. He is concerned about persons and is always aware that each statistic is first of all a person, with hopes, fears, aspirations, needs.

A man, age 43, and his wife, age 40, have nine children, ages 17, 16, 14, 13, 10, 8, 6, 4, and 1. His job pays him $100 a week and he works in a barber shop weekends. They sought the help of their pastor because of discipline problems with the children.

A family in their 40s was living on $50 a week. The wife invited a nephew and his friend to live with them. The husband called the pastor to discuss the problem because of the economic matter as well as the conflict between husband and wife.

These two families represent 15 people who comprise statistics that run into over 20 million.

Poverty in the Midst of Plenty:
The Contemporary Dilemma

One who works with the poor must be conscious of the fact that there is poverty in the midst of plenty and of the problems this creates.

A long time ago Pitt said, "Poverty is no disgrace but it is damned annoying." In America it can be both annoying and a disgrace.

One thing that is different in poverty today from any previous generation is that now poverty is surrounded by so much affluence and plenty.

Poverty is one of the major social issues of our society. It has ramifications that are political, social, economic, personal, pyschological, and spiritual. Urbanization, industrialization, periodic depressions, unemployment, massing people together in huge ghettos, prejudice and discrimination against minorities, underlying unrest, violence and revolt have all combined to create a social issue of mammoth proportions. While this has created a major problem for a large segment of society, the vast majority are enjoying prosperity that is unequaled in any previous generation. This creates all sorts of psychological and emotional tensions.

Perhaps the most difficult problem of all is the apathy of the affluent, the feeling that the more fortunate do not care. The real problem, Stern and De Vincent say, "lies not so much in the not-new *fact* of poverty in the midst of plenty as in the manner in which an increasingly affluent society has forsaken its poor, ignored or excluded them, lost sight of their needs." (*The Shame of a Nation*, p. 21.)

It is characteristic of people to ignore or shut out what they do not want to see. Not that people haven't been concerned about poverty. They have. It has been the subject of endless discussion and debate. An article in the *New York Times* pointed out a lot of people are concerned about poverty, but not many are concerned about the poor.

The pastor must demonstrate that he is concerned about poverty and cares about persons who are poor.

A young man attending college sought his pastor because he hoped to continue his education but had no funds. His mother and father have seven children and no money. The pastor, through the church, was able to secure some funds to assist the young man with his education.

A young woman, whose parents were separated and whose mother lived with the children in a government housing project, wanted a college education. She was the oldest daughter at 18. Because of the help of a pastor, who was able to secure some financial assistance through the church, she was able to go on to school.

The poor are well aware that most people in other parts of town have not only tuition provided by their parents, but cars, clothes, and spending money as well. It is the old question of the "haves" and "have nots." As one man put it, "The haves have everything, the poor have nothing."

Self-Perpetuation of Poverty

One who would work with the poor must recognize that much poverty is self-perpetuating.

This is one of the major tragedies of poverty. Because of their poverty, many people find it difficult to improve themselves. The result is that many families that are poor remain poor for a long time. Many of the children of the poor can expect to stay poor. As one man who knew poverty by first-hand experience said, "Poverty is a vicious cycle. You are born in this cycle and in most cases you die here." The longer an individual or family remains in this condition, the more difficult it is to effect change. Forty percent of those on AFDC (Aid to Families of Dependent Children) had received help when they were children.

During the days of the Depression, though many people were unemployed, even on breadlines, they felt the situation was temporary. People who have been in poverty for the second and third generation feel it is permanent.

Gerald Leinwand says, "Because they are poor, because they have been poor for a long time, many of the poor see no way out of their poverty. The future looks blank and hopeless. The hopelessness of the parents is passed on to the children from generation to generation. Because of the 'facts of poverty' we have come increasingly to realize that the poor cannot be expected to improve themselves through their own efforts alone." (*Poverty and the Poor*, p. 33.)

Much of this is beyond the person's control. The poor are the victims of circumstances. Poor educational systems, racism, welfare systems that enhance rather than ameliorate the situation, the indifference and apathy of the affluent, all continue and perpetuate the tragedy of poverty from one generation to the next.

A pastor made a call at a home in his neighborhood. He found three small children at home alone. All were naked. The house was very dirty, to the point of being filthy. The father had disappeared. The mother had a chance for a job. The children were left to take care of themselves. They needed food and clothing immediately. This kind of problem is rarely found in a pastoral call in suburbia.

"Do the methods described in the books on pastoral care and taught in our seminaries apply in a poverty area? . . ."

III. People and Their Response to Poverty

Differences in Response

One who would work with the poor must understand that people respond differently to poverty.

The people who live in poverty can be described or discussed in many ways. There are the children and the aged, the white, the black, and the brown; there are rural and urban, first generation and second generation, migrants and inhabitants of the ghetto, racial groups and ethnic groups. These are meaningful descriptions, and must be considered if one is to understand the total problem.

John Kenneth Galbraith, in his book *The Affluent Society,*

spoke of "case" poverty and "insular" poverty. Case poverty can exist anywhere, in any community—rural or urban—at any time. It consists of an individual case of poverty (which can be a whole family) which can be due to health, circumstances, or attitude, no matter what the general economic situation may be. It is more an individual problem than a social problem.

Insular poverty is an island of poverty. "In the island everyone or nearly everyone is poor." Whole regions (as in Appalachia), or whole sections of a city (as in the ghetto), or whole groups (as with some Mexican-American groups, American Indians, etc.) are poor. One cannot explain matters by individual inadequacy or a failure to take advantage of opportunities. The total culture of poverty affects everyone in the area.

Another approach is to consider the way people have been affected, the way they have responded to poverty. This applies whether it is case or insular poverty, rural or urban, white, black, or brown.

We have found five different ways that people respond to poverty. Before listing them, we would point out there is no clear line that separates them, nor are they static. Persons may move from one group to another.

(1) There are those who are *redemptively creative*. They have not only risen above poverty, they have actually used it, learned from it, been more useful because of it. Historically there have been many examples. Lincoln was raised in what would be considered rural poverty today. Charles Dickens' father was thrown in a debtors' prison but he used his experiences as the basis for his stories. William Booth was apprenticed at age 13, but as a result of his experience he dedicated his life to the alleviation of suffering and founded the Salvation Army. The list is a long one: Beethoven, Handel, Mme. Curie, Emerson, and more. These are names of people who have attained fame and recognition. There are many who did not publish, establish insitutions, or attain high office who have risen above poverty and been creative and strong.

The percentage of people who are able to triumph over such experiences and use them may be small. There are not many people in any group who are triumphantly creative. How it compares with those in other economic levels who are triumphantly creative is not known.

(2) There are those who meet the situation with courage and strength. These are the *stable* poor. They may not be as creative, but they are in control of the situation. The situation does not control them. Things are tough but they are not crippling. They manifest a sense of humor. They usually have a sense of family strength and religious faith. They may call it "soul" but it sustains them.

(3) There are those who are *coping with* poverty. The problems are tough. At times poverty gets them down, but they come back. They manage to carry on. It is a constant struggle. There are also periods of control and contentment. They are very much influenced by the availability of jobs, sufficient funds for the necessities, etc. There is much discouragement and bitterness, but they are coping with it.

(4) There are those who are burdened by poverty. They are *unstable* economically, socially, emotionally. They experience a continuous struggle in which the defeats outnumber the victories. The problems are too numerous to cope with, their resources are so few, the community support and assistance is so limited that they either depend on others to maintain them or fold in defeat.

(5) There are those who are seemingly defeated. They are *submerged* by poverty. They have withdrawn from the battle, psychologically, emotionally, and behaviorally.

The pastor's task is clear. It is to help a person move to a more courageous and creative response.

While the above statements do describe certain responses that are observable, there are few classifications and no stereotypes that apply to the poor. One young pastor said:

One of the exciting things about working with the poor is that they are always full of surprises. When one expects the poverty-

31

stricken individual to be nonverbal, he speaks freely. When one expects the poor individual to be irresponsible, he acts surprisingly responsible. When it seems that he is at a dead end, the resources of hope and faith bubble up to the surface and he fights his own condition all the more fiercely.

Strengths of the Poor

One who works with the poor must recognize their strengths, utilize them, and build on them.

Most of the studies of the poor stress their problems. Very little is said about their strengths.

One reason the strengths have been overlooked is that those who have written about the poor have been hoping to arouse concern or secure funds. This is best done by emphasizing deprivation, needs, or as one man put it, stressing "the plight of the poor."

The implication has been that this is the total situation and there are no strengths. This is a partial and false impression. Ben Bagdikian, after completing his study, said, "It has been impossible to enter the lives of the poor without realizing how close they are to salvation. They are not, most of them, without spirit and hope." (*In the Midst of Poverty*, p. 12.)

Another reason is that no one has really studied their strengths. There are individuals who have risen above situations of deprivation to a place of usefulness and creativity. This cannot be done without strength.

There are a large number of people who are coping with the situation. People who face tremendous obstacles but are not overcome by them. Bagdikian speaks of those who draw "from morbid circumstances the warmest possible qualities." (*Ibid.*, p. 127.)

For generations it has been religion that has been man's source of strength. This is true in the biblical record, "They who wait for the Lord shall renew their strength." It has been true historically. Many of the poor today are sustained by their religious faith.

The poor manifest unusual courage based on a simple but profound faith. A woman who had experienced great difficulty, economic limitations, and physical pain said to a pastor, "I know God won't let come to us more than we are able to bear. I am going to trust him completely."

Some Common Misconceptions About the Poor

One who would work with the poor must avoid certain common misconceptions about them.

The conception was once widely held that the poor lacked ambition, and were lazy, indifferent, or extravagant. It is now generally recognized that many (if not most) of the poor are poor because of a combination of social and economic circumstances, most of which were beyond their control.

Some feel the poor deserve their fate as a penalty for their sin, their wastefulness, or their idleness. Some have felt that poverty was "good for the soul." They contend that wealth corrupts, but poverty contributes to a simple and wholesome life. A man like Andrew Carnegie contended poverty was necessary to developing greatness.

Some have felt if the poor were helped, they would enjoy being helped, and prefer to stay in poverty rather than to express their own initiative. A common misconception is that the poor are happier and therefore should not be disturbed. Many other myths and misconceptions could be added.

People with a middle-class background often may not take into account either the limited background or facilities of the poor. A man who had been out of work was helped to get a job. He was consistently late. The question was raised, "Why don't you set the alarm clock?" He not only didn't have one, he didn't know what one was, let alone how to work it.

33

"Central to the study was an attempt to understand what took place during actual ministry to persons in need. . ."

IV. The Practical Problems of the Poor

Some of These Problems

One who works with the poor must realize that almost all have multiple practical, economic problems.

The problems of the poor are multiple, practical, and inter-related. They don't have *a* problem; they almost always have problems. They have problems that do not trouble people in affluent America. These are problems that have to do with jobs, food, clothing, housing, medical and dental care, and transportation.

The correlation between poverty and poor health is very

great. The infant mortality rate among the poor is three and a half times that of the rest of the population.

Charles Mayo once said, "Sickness makes people poor; poverty makes people sick." Here begins the vicious cycle. Lack of employment means limited funds. Limited funds mean poor food and an inadequate diet. Poor food means poor health. Poor health means poor performance at school and absenteeism on the job. Poor performance in the job means unemployment. Unemployment means lack of funds. Lack of funds and limited medical care, etc., etc.

Economic disability usually means educational limitations. Educational limitations mean difficulty in securing employment. Unemployment, low wages, means economic disability.

Sometimes these practical problems are so pressing, little else can be accomplished until they are resolved or partially alleviated.

A young woman, age 26, sought help from her pastor. She was separated from her husband, had recently had surgery, sold her house to pay her medical bills, and was in need of funds.

A pastor was counseling with a middle-aged woman who described some physical symptoms that were causing her some concern. He advised that she see a doctor and be treated for them. She saw the doctor and he gave her a prescription. Some time later the pastor asked if the medication was helping; she said she hadn't filled the prescription. When the pastor asked why, she said she couldn't afford it.

The Importance of Housing

One who would work with the poor must recognize the pervasive problem of housing.

Housing has long been recognized as one of the major problems of the poor. There is the economic problem of high rent and low income. The poor probably pay more and get

35

less for their housing than any group in America. There is the personal problem of no privacy, no chance to be alone. There is the prestige problem. One of the things that gives status in our culture is the residence where one lives. Most ghetto housing eats away one's self-image. There is no opportunity for pride in ownership, pride in appearance. There is no sense of permanence or roots. Eviction, urban renewal can force a change of residence overnight.

It is particularly difficult for older persons who find the community changing but who are unable to find new housing because of lack of funds and transportation. The result is many remain isolated in old neighborhoods shut off from friends, unable to get medical attention, to go to church, etc.

The question of housing can be all important. A pastor called on an elderly woman in the county hospital. She was ready to be released but she had no place to go. She was not sick enough to remain in the hospital. She was too sick to live by herself. She had no home, no money, no family, no friends. Housing arrangements were made through the assistance of the Salvation Army.

An elderly woman lives in a one-room shack. She receives $90 from old-age assistance. She owes $300 in back taxes. She either must raise the money, or lose the place; she has nowhere else to go.

The Importance of "Life Space"

One who would work with the poor must be aware of the importance of life space.

Life space is defined as "that part of the city the individual occupies physically, socially and psychologically."

A man like Herbert J. Gains says this is the important factor in housing. He feels that space is more important than rats or holes in the wall in its influence upon the individual. People in a poverty area have almost no individual life space. They have no space that guarantees privacy and solitude, that they can really call their own.

The concept of life space includes not only housing but the whole neighborhood as well. Life space includes the whole functional relationship of the person to the community in which he lives.

A young pastor made a pastoral call in a home. The house consisted of two small rooms. Three generations lived in the two rooms. An elderly man was bedfast, quite ill. Children slept on the floor. The mother of the children had only been able to work a few days a month. Dirty clothes, dirty dishes—filth was everywhere. Cockroaches were all over the floors and walls. The odor of soiled clothing and stale food was very strong. There was no privacy, no place for the children to study, no yard in which to play.

"People in poverty have almost no individual life space, no place that guarantees privacy and solitude, no place they can call their own."

V. Some Psychological Problems of the Poor

Continued Stress

One who would work with the poor must realize they are under almost constant stress.

A person can stand only so much stress. Unemployment and lack of funds mean uncertainty. Uncertainty can create stress. As the cycle of unemployment and lack of funds continues, the stress may be increased. Among the poor the stress is always present. It is almost never relieved.

It is a constant struggle of "trying to make do with a string when a rope is needed." (Shostak and Gomberg, *New Perspective in Poverty*, p. 31.) Continuous stress creates tension.

Tension often produces inefficiency and bitterness. If tension and bitterness continue over a period of time, these have inevitable results in any personality.

A pastor called on a young woman and her five children; all need dental and medical care. She also feeds and clothes a male companion. She fears she will lose him if she doesn't support him but her welfare allowance will not buy enough groceries for the children, let alone another adult. This situation had existed for months and would have continued for months more except the pastor, by offering some firm advice and practical suggestions, was able to help them get medical help and work out some of the personal and financial problems.

A woman, mother of five children, had been badly beaten by her husband several times. She was afraid to live with him but couldn't afford an attorney to get a divorce. She couldn't get a job because she had to care for the children. She needed money for food, she lived in a shack where the roof leaked and they couldn't keep dry in rainy weather and the landlord wouldn't repair it.

The Loneliness of the Poor

One who would work with the poor must be aware of the loneliness of the poor.

Man needs relationships. It is one of the prerequisites for mental health.

Bagdikian describes the plight of the poor, and after listing various problems says, "But the worst ghost of all is loneliness and isolation." (*In the Midst of Plenty*, p. 12.)

Harrington points out that the poor usually do not belong to anything: unions, fraternal organizations, political parties, clubs. "The other America," says he, "is becoming increasingly populated by those who do not belong to anybody or anything." (*The Other America*, p. 18.) It is true there are churches that minister to the poor, but more and more the churches have moved to the suburbs, leaving the religious ministry in the poverty area to the storefront church and an untrained pastor who finds it necessary to work in other employment through the week.

Not all the poor live in cities, but this lack of belonging, this sense of isolation and aloneness, characterizes both the rural and urban poor.

Stern and De Vincent in *The Shame of a Nation*, make the distinction between lonesomeness and aloneness. "Aloneness," they say, "is not knowing which way to turn for help. Aloneness is the helplessness of being caught by forces both incomprehensible and uncontrollable. . . . Above all, aloneness is having no one to join forces with, at any rate not knowing how to join forces with other alone people." (P. 151.) This sense of aloneness permeates the culture of poverty.

A chaplain of Goodwill Industries was talking with one of the workers who said, "Chaplain, I get so tired working during the week, but I always dread the weekend—it's so lonely. It's hard to get back in the groove on Monday mornings but it's better than home."

Another worker asked if he couldn't forego his vacation. He said it was "too lonely" when he wasn't working.

A boy from a poor home had gotten into difficulty. He was embarrassed and somewhat afraid. He said, "I know the kids I run around with don't do what's right, but I want to be accepted."

An elderly man in a poverty area was asked what he missed the most. He replied, "I'd like to go to church. I went a year ago but I don't know when I'll be able to go again. . . . I need a new suit of clothes. I'd like to go to a picture show. This may sound like asking for everything in sight, but I miss things like that. . . . Sure I'd like to be able to walk around without getting dizzy. And go to a picture show. But maybe if I just had some good company, I guess that would be all right too." (Bagdikian, *In the Midst of Plenty*, p. 89.)

Such an illustration points out many things. It points up the problem of the aged poor, who, Harrington says, "live out their lives in loneliness and frustration." (*The Other America,* p. 13.) It expresses a wistful hungering for the fellowship and faith of the church which is not being met. Here is a vast mission field at the church's doorstep. It also points out quite dramatically what a great deal of emotional and spiritual help and strength could be given by a simple pastoral call, whether the call be made by the clergy or the laity, to provide the "company" this man said he misses and needs.

What Bagdikian calls "the lonesome life of the poor" is a challenge to the pastoral ministry and the sense of mission of the church.

The Feeling of Inadequacy

One who would work with the poor must be conscious of the feelings of inadequacy.

Alfred Adler, the famous psychiatrist, said that everyone feels inferior or inadequate to some degree. "To be human is to feel inferior," he said. One of man's chief needs, according to Adler, is to understand these feelings, to redirect their neurotic expression into more wholesome and acceptable channels.

This is difficult for anyone to do. For the person in the poverty area it may be well-nigh impossible. As Bagdikian said, "Poverty invites comparison with others and it is the comparison that produces the sense of failure." (*In the Midst of Plenty,* p. 135.)

All the advertisements on billboards, on television, in magazines and newspapers, glorify new cars, homes, luxuries, washing machines, food—none of which the poor share, none of which they expect to share.

Yet all these things are presented as the average American way of life. Since a poor person does not have them, he may feel he has been denied them, which can produce resentment and bitterness or the feeling he has failed.

For the more affluent such things are at least a possibility. They have had some measure of achievement in school, in the home, on the job. The poor have none of the material evidence of success; they have had few if any experiences of achievement. The result is feelings of inferiority and inadequacy that are deep-rooted and all-pervasive.

J. C. is a young nonprofessional worker in a social agency. He has worked hard to attain his position and functions quite well. He is both pleased and surprised that people express confidence in him. He continually apologizes for his ability and has not accepted some positions that would be considered advances because of his lack of confidence.

Anger

One who would work with the poor must be aware of the unresolved anger.

No one can endure unresolved anger. One can survive without food for a while, one can get along without sex, but one cannot maintain a degree of happiness, contentment, and adjustment if one is continuously angry. Yet economic, political, and social conditions can force the poor to be angry.

No generalization should be applied to all individuals, yet as a group the poor are often angry. They are the victims of injustice, they see the privileges and luxuries of others, they are forced to accept welfare, which makes them feel dependent—all of which fosters anger. It may be suppressed or repressed, but it is there.

A very capable black who read these pages in typescript said, "Anyone who is bright today is angry. Anyone who is bright and poor is angry even more so. Anyone who is bright and poor and black presents a threat to society." If the anger is relieved, it is only for brief periods of time.

Bigger Thomas in *Native Son* said, "I been scared and mad all my life."

Advertisements and TV commercials all invite comparison. Comparison may result in feelings of inadequacy, failure, resentment, and anger. A pastor should expect to meet anger, occasionally even rage.

A man in the emergency room of the county hospital had been cut up pretty badly in a fight. He said to the pastor, "Pray for that other fellow, Reverend, because I'm going to get him. I hope the good Lord takes care of him tonight and that he sleeps real good because I'm going to get him tomorrow."

A man whose wife was in the hospital became very angry at the staff, the attendants, and the chaplain. Three times he was removed from the premises because he was causing trouble. Each time he returned. He said they weren't going to tell him what to do. He said, "I know how they treat blacks at this hospital." When the pastor was able to engage him in conversation, and listened at some length to his complaints, the man's anger subsided somewhat and he apologized for his behavior.

Meaninglessness

One who would work with the poor must be aware of the difficulty of finding meaning in life.

Viktor Frankl, the noted European psychiatrist, stresses in his system of therapy, known as logotherapy, that life has to have meaning. Men must have a goal, a purpose, a faith in the future and meaning in the present. Where meaning, purpose, goals are absent, there can only be frustration and defeat.

Harrington, in his evaluation of the effects of the culture of poverty, says, "The new poverty is constructed so as to destroy aspiration; it is a system designed to be impervious to hope. It is populated by the failures, by those driven from the land and bewildered by the city. . . . Their horizon has become more and more restricted; they see one another, and that means they see little reason for hope." (*The Other America,* pp. 17, 18.)

Yale psychologist Ira Goldenberg said poverty results in "a pattern of hopelessness and helplessness, a view of the world and oneself as static, limited and totally expendable." (Quoted in *Paradox of Poverty in America,* p. 64.)

A young woman who had experienced a combination of problems—economic, moral, family, vocational, and religious—was hospitalized, facing a large debt. In conversation with her pastor she said, "It all seems so meaningless." Her pastor said, "You must get your strength back." She answered, "Why?"

Long-Term Goals

One who would work with the poor can expect to find difficulty in establishing long-term goals.

It is difficult for some in poverty areas to accept or be challenged by long-term goals. They live one day at a time. Their culture and their problems almost force them to focus on the present. Since they have had so little experience with success in the past, it is difficult to look to success in the future.

Some seem to resist improvement. Often it is a certain kind of improvement that is being thrust upon them. What seems to be resistance to improvement may be resistance to middle-class values. Since many pastors have middle-class backgrounds, they may have false expectations of what a person from another cultural group really wants or needs.

Counselors from middle-class backgrounds often think in terms of long-range goals and expect them of their counselees. They can speak to a young person from a middle-class home of the value of planning for a degree he will not receive for four years or more. He can accept this. A person from a poorer home needs so many things right now that he cannot think four or five years ahead. Besides, none of his friends or family are well educated and he may doubt that it will do him any good if he is. Both counselor and counselee feel frustrated in such a situation. One sees education as essential, almost as a way of life. The other does not feel it is a basic need at all.

A woman was in need of funds. She had never had a job. She seemed willing to work, but did not know how to apply. She was helped to get a job in a laundry. She worked for a few days, received some money, and quit. She had had no experience of success in the past, and she saw no need of planning for the future.

"Problems of the poor are almost always multiple, interrelated, economic and emotional—all of which are very practical and need immediate attention."

VI. Special Areas and Special Groups Among the Poor

The Elderly

One who would work with the poor must be aware of the needs of the elderly.

One specialist in geriatrics said most elderly people feel unwanted and most of them are right. This is particularly true of the elderly poor. Many of the 8 million elderly poor feel neither wanted nor needed. Our culture is difficult enough for all older persons. It can be almost overwhelming for the poor.

Their problems are a mixture of the practical, the economic, the psychological, and the spiritual.

Housing and life space are important for everyone but very difficult for the elderly. Older persons are often the victims of circumstances, having very little to say about where they live. One study of the elderly indicated over 90 percent were unhappy with their living arrangements.

Many are continuing to exist in unsatisfactory situations because they cannot afford anything better. They do not have the transportation to look for other arrangements. It requires great effort to pack even their limited belongings and move. They do not want to leave familiar surroundings even though the community has changed.

Older persons find it difficult to travel; buses are hard to get on, and many trips require a transfer. As a result, many do without needed medical and dental care, do not do the shopping for groceries that are needed, and do not get to church simply because doctors' offices, supermarkets, and churches are hard to get to. Many of the elderly poor seldom get outdoors, seldom meet other people, live on Social Security or dwindling pensions, and are unknown to churches and even neighbors.

Many are placed in old-age homes, convalescent homes, and other institutions because there are no families or friends to care for them. Some receive kindly treatment; many do not. In some cases the names of the residents of the homes are hardly known to the staff that is responsible for their care. "A resident of the old age home must foster the illusion that he is among the living, although awareness that he has been discarded by relatives, friends and society is not uncommon." (*Paradox of Poverty in America,* p. 54.)

Of all the groups in a poverty area, perhaps the problems of the elderly poor are the most difficult. A man who had worked closely with the poor, especially with blacks, said, "Saddled with high drug and doctor bills, dependent on fixed incomes that do not rise with raising prices, the aged are caught in a morass of despair." Then he added, "Being poor, elderly, and forgotten may be the worst fate of all."

An elderly woman, 87 years of age, lived alone. She had no relatives, no close friends. She did have a small home. She was willing to deed the home to someone who would come and stay with her so she would not be alone. She called her pastor for help, but he could not find anyone either.

An elderly man, 83 years of age, was taken to the hospital because he was found lying in the street. He had been drinking, and had fallen and broken his nose. The pastor had to communicate by writing on a scratch pad because he was deaf. The pastor took him to a dingy flat where he lived alone. The pastor found he was not receiving any welfare assistance, helped him apply and find a much more pleasant and suitable apartment.

Children of the Poor

One who would serve people in poverty should give special attention to the children.

A long time ago Jacob Riis wrote a book called *The Children of the Poor.* His purpose was to awaken the public conscience to this great area of need in American society. A lot has happened since Riis published his book. The problem of the children of the poor is still with us. According to the *Encyclopedia of Social Work,* one fourth of all the children in America live in poverty.

What is said about poverty in general and its effect on man's outlook applies doubly to children. It can twist and deform the spirit; it is destructive to both aspiration and hope. "The hopelessness of the parents is passed on to the children from generation to generation." (*Poverty and the Poor,* p. 33.)

The incidence of disease among children in poverty is tragically greater than in the rest of society. It is true there are programs of child welfare that are designed to meet the needs of children, but it is estimated that AFDC funds reach only about one out of six of the impoverished children, and this deals almost exclusively with physical welfare.

It is one thing to quote figures of the millions that are in poverty, the 400,000 whose parents work and who are left to shift for themselves. It is another thing to minister to one such child in his loneliness and illness.

A pastor was particularly concerned about children and volunteered to work in the children's ward of a charity hospital. The pastor was a woman who related well with children.

One of the children she saw was a Mexican-American girl aged 9. She was a friendly, open child who responded to attention. Some of the hospital personnel called her a "demanding child."

In answer to questions about the family, she had a stock answer, "I forgot a hundred years ago."

She was Catholic and the pastor was Protestant, and there was some difficulty in establishing any identity other than that of someone who was interested in her—nothing is more important, especially if there aren't many people who are interested.

On one occasion the child pointed out that even her mother hadn't visited for over a week. On this same visit she said she wished the ward was empty so she would have all the attention and all the toys. It was the same visit that she took a dime from a plastic bank and attempted to give it to the pastor. The pastor said, "She never wants me to go—and begs me to stay or grabs my arm."

A pastor was called to the emergency room of the county hospital at 2:00 A.M. A 14-year-old boy was there for treatment. He wouldn't let the doctor or the nurse touch him until the pastor arrived and said it was okay. He did not even know the pastor but knew some young people who were in his church. Later conversation revealed he was one of sixteen children living with his mother who was attempting to support the children. He was related to the youth program at the church and became a part of it.

The Mentally Ill

A pastor who works with the poor will find many who are mentally or emotionally disturbed.

Most of the studies of mental illness in the population as a whole indicate there is a higher percentage of mental illness among the poor than in the rest of society. Such studies also indicate that mental illness among the poor takes different forms from those in suburbia. The poor are more likely to have hysterical psychoses and hysterical conversion reactions associated with belief in magic in various forms. Neurotic and psychotic expressions among the poor are more likely to take the form of violence rather than psychosomatic illness and functional disorders which would be characteristic of suburbia.

Research also points out that there are more neurotics among the affluent, more psychotics among the poor. This may be due to the fact that the psychotics attract attention and receive treatment; the neurotics do not. Since the data for such comparisons are usually collected from treatment files, this raises many questions as to their inclusiveness. How many neurotics do not receive treatment in poverty areas? Or in suburbia, for that matter? (*Psychological Factors in Poverty*, p. 243.)

The study that is quoted most frequently is the Midtown Manhattan study conducted in the sixties. In this study information was collected from 1,660 adults who were randomly selected. The data were evaluated by two psychiatrists on a six-point scale. The scale ranged from "well" to "incapacitated." It was found that there was a high correlation between socio-economic status and mental health. "Well" ratings decreased, and "incapacitated" increased as one went down the economic scale. It was noted that there was a definite increase in mental disturbance when one reached the edge-of-poverty group, and again at the chronic poverty level.

While studies such as these are generally confirmed in experience and accepted as being characteristic of communities in general, they have been subject to some question because the type of evaluative decision or diagnoses that have been made are somewhat biased if not judgmental in nature; that is, they are subject to the value judgments of the raters, who are almost never poor. Behavior which they consider neurotic or sick may be very adaptive in the lower-class culture. Personality measures which would be appropriate in middle-class society may not be appropriate with the poor.

Some things are obvious from all such studies as well as from observation. The more stress factors are present, the greater the proportion of mental impairment. The culture of poverty can increase and intensify stress, as is pointed out elsewhere in these pages. It is only to be expected, therefore, that one will find a higher incidence of mental illness here than elsewhere.

One of the most important factors is that treatment is more difficult to secure, and in some cases almost nonexistent, in a poverty area. Psychiatric treatment is time-consuming and expensive. Counseling services are limited.

The result is that the poor receive less treatment for such disorders than any segment of society, and there is almost no psychotherapy. The poor are usually treated at a mental health clinic, as out-patients of a county hospital, in the psychiatric unit of a county hospital, or in a state hospital. In most cases they are treated by chemotherapy, although some clinics and hospitals provide individual and group psychotherapy.

The pastor is not concerned about statistics except as they reveal trends. He is concerned about persons, and he knows many of the people he ministers to have real mental and emotional problems. He needs to be able to detect them, especially in the early stages. He needs to know when medical and psychiatric referral is indicated and when it isn't. He needs to know the referral resources in his community and how to help persons accept and receive help. He can also help the person's family to understand the nature of the problem and how they can help. While the sick person is in the hospital, the pastor can show his concern and provide a link with the church and the outside world. He can also be of real service when the discharged patient returns to the community by assisting him in the rehabilitation process. Clifford Beers said a long time ago, "What the mentally ill person most needs ia a friend." The pastor can be that friend.

A young man was discharged from his job because he couldn't get along with other workers. He lost several jobs in succession, became more withdrawn, more hostile, more melancholy and discouraged. The pastor suggested he go to the state mental health clinic to get their evaluation and some possible medication, and agreed to continue to see him and work with him.

A 76-year-old woman was found in a bar dancing on one of the tables. She did not know who she was, where she lived, or if she had any relatives. She gave several names which she said might have been hers, and several people who might be her relatives, but she wasn't sure. She seemed quite disoriented. She didn't know if she had a home or not. She was taken to the Salvation Army, who provided housing and food until she could receive treatment.

The Alcoholic and the Poor

One who would work with the poor will see some who have escaped by drinking.

Alcoholism is present in all levels of society. In a poverty area it is more likely to be complicated by a "Skid Row" section consisting of homeless men whose problems are accentuated by their lack of roots, lack of occupational skills, lack of motivation together with chronic physical disease, mental illness, and frequent arrests.

Some of them frequent missions and the Salvation Army because they provide food and lodging, with a strong dose of religion. The number of cures is small. Some missions do report conversions that have produced sobriety. Such missions also aid in securing jobs. The pastor would do well to utilize all the resources of medicine, Alcoholics Anonymous and the church.

A middle-aged woman, highly intoxicated, was taken to the hospital. The pastor called her husband to come and take her home. He was intoxicated also. She said she had been drinking a long time, ever since she had problems with her parents. It is worse since her 19-year-old daughter rejected her. She accepted referral to Family Service and AA. The husband refused any referral.

A middle-aged woman was highly intoxicated when the pastor called at the request of the police. She admitted being an alcoholic, had belonged to AA but quit. She expressed concern about her husband, who disapproved of her drinking. She said, "I am lost. I don't know what to do. My husband doesn't know what to do either." She also said she knew a drunkard couldn't enter the kingdom of heaven. Her present condition began because of lack of funds and cataracts on her eyes which prevented her getting a job. The pastor arranged a referral to a doctor and to the Medicaid program so her cataracts could be removed. He also referred her to Family Service, which in turn related her to another AA group and to a job placement center. Through it all was an extended discussion of the nature of a loving God who relates to all people, no matter who they are. This relieved her guilt and gave much reassurance.

The Problems of Men

One should be particularly sensitive to the problems of men among the poor.

Men are not usually considered a minority group, especially in these days of women's liberation, but men in the culture of poverty do have unique problems. The culture of poverty particularly downgrades the male. A man who does not work loses his self-respect, the respect of the community, and the respect of his own children. The simple fact is in time of unemployment a woman can find marginal jobs easier than a man. This is particularly true among blacks, where men are often unemployed. As one man in a poor community said, "How can a man pull himself up by his own bootstraps when he hasn't got any boots?"

When the wife goes to work and the man stays at home, it reverses the expected roles. The wife may assume dominant attitudes. The children go to the mother instead of the father for money, advice, or guidance. The loss of self-esteem on the part of the male is common.

A man had been out of work for thirty days. He was too proud to seek welfare. He was not a member of any church, but he went to a pastor to see if he could borrow $25. He offered to join the church if he could get the loan.

A man and his wife had several children and cared for some from the wife's previous marriage. She could find steady employment keeping house for a physician. He stayed home and took care of the children. This reversal of cultural roles is hard for some to accept.

The Sick

One who works with the poor should give special attention to the sick.

The incidence of disease among the poor is many times higher than in suburbia, which may be only a few blocks away. A study in Chicago showed that infant mortality in the slums was three times higher than in other parts of the city. Many do not receive any medical or dental care at all. When they do, it is usually at a county hospital where they are placed in an overcrowded ward, or in the out-patient queues, waiting hours for their turn to be seen briefly by a doctor or a nurse. This is not without some value. It provides a degree of fellowship and diversion from the monotony of the rest of their lives. One psychiatrist said it would be very unfortunate if county hospitals became efficient and had sufficient staff to handle these people in a hurry. They would lose a lot of value from the trip.

Some of the diseases found in a poverty area, such as rickets, scurvy, beri-beri, and pellagra, are hardly known in other parts of town. Some medical students do not even know they exist.

Illness is always an emotional, spiritual experience as well as a physical one. Only a few have a pastor of their own. If the hospital provides a chaplain, he must divide his day to meet the needs of several hundred patients.

A pastor doing volunteer calling under the auspices of the chaplains' office of the county hospital simply identified himself as a pastor. He kept a record of the people's response to such an introduction. Repeatedly they would say, "Pray for me." "Remember me in your prayers," etc.

A woman whose husband had been shot was in the waiting room of the emergency room of the county hospital. When asked if there was anything she wanted, she said she "wanted a preacher."

A woman whose husband had been ill said afterward, "You don't know how much my pastor meant to me." Perhaps his ministry to her was as effective as his ministry to the patient.

A young man had a serious illness and was treated at the county hospital. The attending physician said his recovery was due to his personal strength, good nursing care, and his pastor's attention.

Other Groups

One who works with the poor will find many people with special needs.

There are many other special areas which could be included and discussed. Each one deserves a chapter or a volume in itself. Each one represents vast numbers of human need.

The rural poor. It is often assumed that poverty is concentrated in ghettos, but 8 million of the nation's poor live on the farm. A rural slum can be just as barren as an urban one. Farmers and farm workers are among the most debt-ridden in America. They face the hard fact that many are not needed anymore.

The transient and migratory workers. Nobody really knows how many of these people there are. They are constantly on the move with no community ties, no funds, no vocational skills. They represent all ages and all races. They may be among the most impoverished and receive less help than any group.

The handicapped. This includes many varieties and many degrees: the visually handicapped, the deaf, the orthopedically handicapped, those with speech disorders, and others. The tragedy is that some of their handicaps could be corrected and others improved if they had funds and knew resources were available.

The retarded. Poverty is difficult to cope with by anyone. When one has limited mental capacity it is next to impossible. The prevalence of retardation appears to be greater among those with low income. It is not known how much of this is due to environmental influences, or the fact that the poor get less professional care and have fewer educational opportunities. But among the poor there is a higher percentage of those who receive less specialized assistance than others.

The gifted. Strange as it may sound, these may be the most neglected and misunderstood of all. They are vast in intellectual potential, but their abilities may be unchallenged, their potential undeveloped, and their personal growth thwarted and unrealized. Many are undiscovered, their possibilities unrecognized by home or school. Ambitions toward higher education may be questioned, even ridiculed or opposed, by family and friends. The result is society loses the benefits of their contributions and they never realize the fulfillment of which they are capable. Some by virtue of their own strength and courage rise to eminence. There is no way to know how many poor people who had great ability were not able to secure the education and training necessary to develop or apply their ability. This is a tragic waste.

Each of these groups needs a ministry. All too few receive it.

A severely crippled young man, heavily in debt and on welfare, was attempting to learn a new skill. His physical handicap limited his progress and resulted in many failures. He said to his pastor, "Sometimes I wonder if it is worth it. There is no future. . . . I really wonder."

In a sheltered workshop for the retarded, all of whom were poor, a series of fights broke out between the workers. When interviewed by a pastor, who was chaplain to the agency, one of them said, "Oh, I don't know what's wrong, chaplain. It's just that everything's been going wrong. Nothing's right and I can't do nothing to make things right. It makes me so damn mad."

A young man wanted to talk to a pastor about some things he had been thinking. He had been reading Camus, and other authors of equal depth, and couldn't find anyone with whom to discuss the ideas.

Minority Groups

One who would work with the members of minority races should expect some resistance, even hostility.

An unduly large proportion of the poor are members of minority races. This does not mean the majority of the poor are black or brown. They are not. It is estimated that 60 to 70 percent of all people living in poverty are white. What it does mean is that a greater percentage of members of minority races are poor. Unemployment among blacks is twice that of whites, for example.

The largest of the minority groups are the blacks. This is their one conspicuous characteristic—their color—and it doesn't change. Irish, Italians, and Poles once experienced prejudice and discrimination too. However, by education and effort they could move up in the educational and social scale and escape unfair treatment. The Negro, no matter how much he achieves, still faces discrimination and prejudice. Thus the problems of poverty are compounded by race.

Other minority groups—such as the Mexican-Americans in the Southwest, the Puerto Ricans in New York, the American Indians, on and off the reservations—all have their struggle with poverty. To discuss them adequately would require a volume for each, written by one who was familiar with their cultural values, their unique problems and needs. While they have much in common, they all are different.

The problems of a black living in a matriarchal culture is different from a Mexican-American in a patriarchal society. Unless the pastor is aware of the cultural mores of the group with which he is working, he will not only be ineffective, he will probably arouse resistance and hostility when these cultural patterns are ignored or misunderstood.

Julian Fast, in his book *Body Language,* tells of a Puerto Rican girl who was being interviewed by a school authority, along with several other girls, for breaking school rules. She claimed innocence but because she refused to look him in the eye, he felt she was being evasive and dishonest. Later he was informed that in Puerto Rican culture a "good girl" does not look an adult in the eye. Not to do so is a sign of respect and obedience.

People who have been subjected to prejudice, injustice, exploitation find it difficult to express their feelings to anyone, let alone someone who is a representative of the group that has exploited him. No matter how understanding the pastor may be, he may be rendered ineffective simply because he is of another color. This makes it difficult to counsel with members of another race.

Also minority groups feel their minority status so deeply they may not want to discuss problems with anyone other than their own group. If a person is extremely militant, he may see the other person as an enemy.

On the other hand, it has been done. White pastors have helped black people. Black pastors have helped white people. If one can gain the confidence and trust of the other person, race is not of too much significance.

If a pastor is to work with members of another race, he must be aware of his own prejudices and his own feelings.

A young white pastor had accepted a position as chaplain in a social agency in the poorest part of town. He expressed considerable concern as he approached his assignment. He described his experience in these words: 'By that time I had arrived, walked into the agency with some hesitation, and realized that my worst fears had come true. I was the only white man in the room! As I met each of the workers, all the fears and anxieties which were mine communicated themselves through extra wet palms, an over-eager "how do you do," dry mouth, and stumbling speech patterns. How did I know these feelings were being communicated? I knew by the way various people met me. Some let their anger toward whites show. Obviously this produced more fear in me. Others were indifferent, and still others made very kind concessions to put me at ease." Fortunately he was able to work through these feelings and established such a relationship that he could not only counsel with the clients of the agency, but the staff as well, all of whom were of another race.

A young pastor was asked to work with a Mexican-American boy at the request of the school authorities. The pastor was new to the community (in the Southwest). It was his first contact with Mexican-Americans. The boy was in constant trouble at school, went out of his way to pick fights, carried a knife and on occasion had used it. Only when the pastor learned the meaning of *machismo* to a Mexican-American did he begin to understand the boy.

"The hopelessness of the parents is passed on to the children—yet in the children there is hope."

VII.   The Church and Poverty

The Absence of the Church

A pastor who would work with the poor must realize that the church is subject to criticism for its seeming avoidance of the poor.

The church has been criticized for abdicating its responsibilities for the poor and retreating to the suburbs. Like all criticism this is not entirely fair. Some pastors and some churches are attempting to minister to the poor. Several are described in these pages.

But some criticism of the church is justified. One author says very bluntly, "The fact that the church is out of touch with the poor of our land is not merely a problem of ignorance but one of deliberate commitment. Christians, like others, choose willfully to be aloof from human need. We consciously remove ourselves from the problem of poverty by the manner in which we become committed to a middle class style of life." (Simon, *Faces of Poverty*, p. 109.)

The absence of the church from the needs of the poor may be the result of complete geographical relocation. The church separates itself from the needs of the people by relocating in a community where such problems are not present. It is also possible for the church to remain in a poverty area geographically but still be "absent" in the sense that it does not demonstrate genuine concern.

In the heat of a family argument a woman shot her husband. There was a great deal of confusion as a result of the sound of the shot. Later the sound of the sirens of police and ambulance drew the usual crowd. Children needed to be cared for. Neighbors tried to help as best they could. All this took place within easy hearing of a church which was having a meeting. What the nature of the meeting was is not known. No one from the church attempted to help. Next day, by request, the pastor did call to see about the children.

The Culture of Poverty and the Church

Pastors who would work with the poor should expect extreme reactions to the church and its ministry.

Many in poverty areas have had only a superficial and limited contact with the church, and some have had none at all. They have almost no knowledge of religious teachings or religious experience to draw upon. They do not know what to expect of a pastor.

The church in the minds of many is identified with the middle and upper class that has exploited or patronized the poor and minorities, and it is rejected with all the rest of the so-called Establishment. Anyone representing the church starts with a disadvantage with such people.

The fact also must be recognized that the established

churches to a large extent have abandoned the poverty areas in most cities and moved to the suburbs.

On the positive side, many of the poor have had a valuable, meaningful relationship with the church. For generations the church has been a source of comfort and strength to the poor and to the disadvantaged.* They have known pastors who were limited in training but had deep compassion and would give of themselves sacrificially in service to their people. A pastor produces very positive responses from such persons.

On occasion repressed hostility may be directed to a pastor. A pastor called on a woman in the county hospital. He introduced himself as Pastor _____ and said, "Is there anything I can do to help?" She said, "As far as I know you're a policeman. You're all alike. You're not going to take advantage of me. The police would just as soon kill you as not! I don't want anything to do with you."

A young woman, a member of the church, called her pastor to discuss a problem about her 12-year-old son. He is a talented musician and has played at the church since he was 8 years old. A night club operator offered him a job entertaining at a night club. Because they were poor he wanted to earn the money. The mother was fearful that he might "forget God" if he did.

Religious Beliefs and Expressions

One who works in the culture of poverty should expect a wide variety of religious expressions and beliefs.

A pastor who has been raised in a traditional, historic branch of the church and trained in a typical theological

---

* Some of the blacks who read the manuscript in typescript raised a question here. They felt the church had also had a negative influence in that its emphasis on "everything will get better by and by" had actually inhibited efforts for change and kept people poor. While we recognize the reality of their position, this does not take away the fact that the church has also been a source of comfort and strength.

seminary will find many religious beliefs that are strange and unfamiliar among the poor. Few people in poverty areas have had the benefit of consistent religious training. Very few read religious literature. Their religious beliefs may be a mixture of traditional Protestant and Catholic theology, regular denominational positions, cult beliefs, and liberal and conservative ideas, sometimes combined with elements of superstition and magic.

At the same time one often finds deep personal expressions of religious faith that are an explanation for the courage, confidence, and joy that are found there.

A Mexican-American who had received help with food and clothing made the statement that the percentage of black magic had gone up. The pastor asked if he felt he had been cursed by black magic and he answered, "Of course. Why would I be here with this problem if I hadn't been cursed?" When asked who put the curse on him, he replied that he didn't dare tell or another curse would be put on him that "would be twice as bad."

A Continuing Ministry

People who live in a poverty area have rarely experienced a sustained or continuing ministry.

The longer a pastor lives in a community, and the better he knows his people, the easier it is to establish a relationship of trust. A long pastorate is very rare in a poverty community. The neighborhood church concept largely has been lost. It is unusual for any workers, religious or secular, to stay for long periods of time. People do not expect the pastor to stay very long. They have been disappointed so many times before, why risk establishing a relationship that will only lead to another disappointment?

One woman put it this way. "We're not worth helping for long. They come in and do their good thing and then when they are satisfied with themselves they are gone. They really don't care about the people."

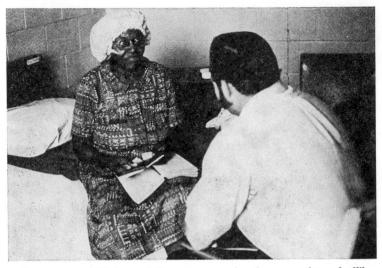

"Being poor, elderly, and forgotten may be the worst fate of all"—unless one is remembered.

VIII. Pastoral Care, Pastoral Counseling, and the Poor

Pastoral Care and Poverty: A Blind Spot

One who would work with the poor will find very little guidance in the literature on pastoral care and counseling.

The pastoral care movement has been one of the most vital and significant emphases in the church in recent years. It has challenged and prepared pastors to recognize the personal, emotional, and spiritual needs of their people and to minister to them in very effective ways. A whole library of literature has been developed that includes discussions of counseling techniques, methods of pastoral care, how to understand and minister to the sick, the elderly, and the family. Very little in the pastoral care literature deals with the disadvantaged or the poor. In this area the pastor is largely on his own as far as printed material on either principles or methods is concerned.

We surveyed the literature rather carefully and found only occasional references to poverty or the poor in the books on pastoral care, and a few articles in religious journals such as *Pastoral Psychology*. We asked a group of pastors working in poverty areas to read some basic books on pastoral care and evaluate them as to their practical help in this area. The response was varied. Some found them helpful; others thought they had limited value. (A bibliography of books and articles on pastoral care is listed in Appendix F.)

We also studied the literature on poverty as such. Most of it was prepared by sociologists, social workers, and journalists. While it proved to be very helpful in understanding poverty, it very rarely made mention of a pastor or offered suggestions as to how he can help. (A selective bibliography of books on poverty of interest to the pastor is found in Appendix F.)

The truth is, no one really knows enough to speak authoritatively on pastoral counseling or pastoral care in poverty areas.

Counseling and the Culture of Poverty

One who would work with the poor should expect not only hesitation but resistance to the counseling or pastoral care.

People in poverty areas have an intense distrust of the middle and upper classes in general. This makes it difficult for them to relate to pastors or counselors who represent these groups.

If the counselee is young and the counselor is over thirty, you add the fact that teen-agers have a distrust of adults in general. When you add this to the cultural factor, the problem is compounded.

If the counselee is black or brown and the counselor is

white, you introduce still a third component into the relationship.

In each case it is difficult for the counselee to accept the counselor as one who can help.

A parishioner asked her pastor to call on a neighbor because she could hear children crying. When the pastor called he found a house with no windows. It was midwinter and there were no utilities. The children were in need of food and clothing. The mother was a young woman whose husband was in jail. Another man was living there. When the pastor offered his services to help the children, she refused, saying it was none of his business what happened to her children. By patiently accepting her resentment he finally was able to obtain help for the children.

Motivation for Counseling

One who works with the poor should expect different motivations for counseling than he finds in the middle class.

It is recognized that the counselee's motivation in seeking counseling, his desire for change, is a very influential factor in all counseling procedures.

Two factors are present in every counseling situation: the skill and understanding of the counselor and the motivation of the counselee. Of the two, the latter is probably the more important. When a person has a trusting relationship with his counselor, when he understands and believes in the counseling process, when he is motivated to make a genuine effort because he feels (expects) that growth and change are possible, then some success is almost automatic. These are precisely the things that are difficult for the person in poverty to attain.

He views the counselor with some suspicion. He does not have either knowledge of, or confidence in, the counseling procedure. He is very doubtful that any change is possible, and hence may have little motivation to put forth the effort.

A long time ago Freud said, "We shall probably discover that the poor are even less ready to part with their neuroses than the rich, because the hard life that awaits them when they recover has no attraction, and illness in them gives them more claim to the help of others."

Conceptions of Counseling

One who works with the poor should expect them to have different conceptions of counseling than do middle- or upper-class persons.

Counseling depends on the pastor's having confidence in his methods and the counseling procedure. It is also important that the counselee understands both the counselor's role and his own. He needs to know what is expected of him and what he should do to facilitate the counseling process. Many people who seek counseling are confused and lacking in understanding as to what they should do or say. This is true in all segments of society. It is especially true in poverty areas. Counseling is almost totally unfamiliar to them. Many are unfamiliar with the word.

People in the middle class have been used to a whole series of relationships with professionals. They have gone to doctors and dentists; they have known teachers and pastors who have been willing to help. Many of these relationships are highly verbal in nature. The people in poverty sections have had very few such experiences. The experience of talking about problems is not familiar to them. Their idea of help probably is someone who does something for them—something quite practical and specific.

A pastor was discussing a problem with a young man who had sought his help. The pastor offered what he felt was a good "Christian" solution. The response he got was, "Man, that's nice, but it's crazy; it'll never work." He wanted something specific, practical, and immediate.

A young woman, mother of three children, was married to a man who was the stepfather of the children. She receives no child support. Her present husband fights with her and prevents her from coming to church. She called her pastor to know "God's will" for her life.

Methods of Pastoral Care

One who would work with the poor should expect to use different methods from those he would use in suburbia, or with middle-class or upper-class people.

Some of the methods that have proved useful with middle-class persons have been found ineffective in poverty areas. Howard Clinebell states it this way: "Ministers who serve inner-city or working-class churches soon discover that both the *methods* and the *goals* of pastoral counseling, as usually conceived, are ineffective with many persons from lower socio-educational groups. The goals borrowed from psychotherapy —growth through self-awareness, personality integration through resolving inner conflicts, and movement toward self-fulfillment—are alien to the 'world' of the majority of these persons. (*Basic Types of Pastoral Counseling*, p. 152.)

This does not mean to imply that all techniques and procedures must be changed. Some procedures, such as listening, reflecting feelings, and interpretation, prove useful here also. But one should not be surprised if at times they are ineffective and other techniques are indicated.

A man, 68 years of age, had his car stolen while visiting his wife at the county hospital. Three days later it was found, stripped of everything including the motor. An error was found in his insurance policy. The man thought it included fire and theft— actually it didn't. The agent admitted it was his fault but said there was nothing he could do. The pastor accompanied the elderly gentleman to the insurance company, persuaded them of their responsibility, and the company made full restitution. Without the intervention of the pastor it probably would not have been accomplished.

A man and wife, age 35 and 33, respectively, sought help from their pastor because finances were causing a problem in the home. Actually their income was rather large in comparison with others in the neighborhood and the congregation. The pastor worked out a plan that would curb buying on impulse, eliminated many things that were not needed. The wife was helped to purchase more economically for the kitchen. All debts were consolidated with one monthly payment and a plan devised for getting out of debt. Here the pastor served as a guide and instructor.

Some Modifications in Traditional Counseling Procedures

One who would work with the poor should make some modifications in traditional counseling procedures.

Counseling will usually be more specific, more direct, and will consist of more advice and suggestions.

Counseling will be more action-oriented; the people need and expect immediate results. Help very often may take the form of physical assistance, such as providing bail, getting food stamps, fixing a hole in the roof, or finding housing, before the pastor can do any counseling *per se* or speak of God's love. Change may not be dramatic, but some results need to appear soon.

Counseling will be strongly supportive, undergirding the poor in their difficulties.

A woman was required to serve on jury duty which necessitated being away from work. Her employer refused to pay, although her contract indicated he should. She was quite poor and needed the money. The pastor was sought to see if he might intercede.

A woman was discharged from the county hospital. She needed a job. After a series of applications and refusals she had the op-

69

portunity to become a "stripper" at a night club. Her question was, since no other jobs were available, should she accept the job. She wanted an immediate answer.

T. was a 26-year-old Mexican-American. He was married and had one daughter who had the measles. His wife was pregnant. His car was in an accident and he lost his license. He had to walk more than two hours to his job as a bus boy. He only worked three days a week, which was not sufficient for food and rent. He had gone to county welfare for assistance but didn't have the proper papers so they couldn't help. The woman's group of a church provided food for the family until another solution could be reached. This man needed immediate practical help before any other form of ministry could be effective.

Standing By

One who would minister to the poor should recognize the importance of "standing by."

There are times when the problems of the poor are so complex, the situation is so uncertain and discouraging, the pastor, after exploring all possibilities for help, just "stands by them" in the experience. This is true of all pastoral care, but it is particularly true in poverty areas. There are so few people who can and will stand by.

The pastor goes with the person as he goes to an agency seeking help; he stands by the person and his family in the hospital, at the jail, before the draft board, as he seeks legal aid, in the office of public housing, etc.

One should never minimize the spiritual and therapeutic experience of having someone who is standing by.

A pastor by his presence can offer some support and encouragement. A family who had gone through a time of family stress and illness thanked their pastor for "being with them." They said, "We felt we were not alone." The support of his presence probably meant far more than he realized.

The Place of Counseling

One who would counsel in poverty areas must adapt himself to all sorts of conditions and locations.

Counseling in poverty areas takes place everywhere—in homes, on porches, in hospital corridors, at social agencies, on street corners. People in poverty areas do not think of making an appointment for such and such an hour at the church office. This is a middle-class concept. Offices, providing quiet, privacy, freedom from interruption, are often not available. This is often of more concern to the pastor than it is to the person. The poor are not used to privacy or quiet.

In fact the poor are not accustomed to going into offices at all except for welfare checks, loans, or for police or legal matters. Because of the unpleasant nature of some of these experiences they may be negatively conditioned about being in an office at all.

The pastor of a small church in a borderline community has a small office just off the sanctuary. The services are well attended. The sanctuary is filled if not crowded. During the Sunday school hour and the time between Sunday school and church service the pastor sits in the study. Several people come by. The conversations are usually brief, personal, and practical. He explained, "Most of the people work during the week. They can't come by to discuss their problems then, so they do it on Sunday morning."

People seek pastors, at least some pastors. They wouldn't say they are going for counseling. They would say they want some help.

"Counseling in a poverty area takes place everywhere—in homes, on porches, in hospital corridors, on street corners."

IX. Communication, Counseling, and the Poor

Talk Orientation and Verbal Fluency

One who would work with the poor should not expect a great deal of fluency or "talk orientation."

An article in the *American Personnel and Guidance Journal* pointed out that "fluency is rare with working-class people; most of them communicate with great economy of language." Thus it stressed how this can be very frustrating to the traditionally trained counselor who feels counseling has not been successful "unless their clients verbalize their feelings fluently."

People in poverty areas have immediate practical concerns. They do not see how "just talking about" a problem can help. As Clinebell puts it, "Introspective methods of counseling seem like a waste of time to the person whose particular culture, unlike the middle class, does not condition him to look within to find help. . . . Goals like insight, self-actualization, personality growth are foreign to his style of communicating and irrelevant to his understanding of what he needs." (*Basic Types of Pastoral Counseling*, pp. 15, 23.)

This does not say that everyone refuses to talk, or that catharsis or talking out a problem with people in these areas has no value. This still provides release of emotions. It helps the pastor to understand the person's problem. It provides an opportunity for support. It will probably need to be accompanied by some advice, specific suggestions, and maybe practical help of a direct or material nature.

This hidden language is understood before the children of the poor go to school. For many in the early grades, it is much more common and meaningful than that which is taught in the English classes. For the child or young person it is often the primary language at home and in the community. When the child gets to school, or goes to other parts of town, he may seem inarticulate. The language that is very meaningful for him does not communicate at all to those outside his cultural group. This, of course, may be one of its chief values. It is one way he can preserve his sense of identity, and thwart and deceive those outside.

This "hidden language" varies in different parts of the country. Some words are peculiar to areas such as Watts; some words are used almost nationally. Some words become popular and become a part of general conversation in all groups, and some words have a short history and are dropped. Some words are more common with racial groups, some with age levels, some with institutions such as reform schools.

A pastor who would work among the poor should understand how these words are used. Unless the pastor understands something of the "hidden language of the poor," he will miss the meaning of some important statements. It is considered unwise, however, for one not in this culture to attempt to speak it. One should only use language in which he can converse with confidence and comfort. The pastor who tries to use the language of another group usually hinders communication rather than helps it. It makes him look either patronizing or foolish.

A young black high school graduate got a job but was laid off. Difficulty in finding work left him very frustrated and completely without funds. He was shot in the shoulder in a tavern scuffle, which left him partially paralyzed in the left arm. A long hospitalization meant more frustration. During this time a pastor called and listened. He made an occasional comment, acknowledging that "it was rough." Later the young man said, "I'm glad there was someone who would listen to me."

Communication and the Hidden Language of the Poor

One who would work with the poor should anticipate difficulties in communication and make efforts to resolve them.

All pastoral counseling and pastoral care is dependent on communication. Communication takes many forms, both verbal and nonverbal. It includes facial expression, tone of voice, bodily actions—but most of all language.

Communication through language only takes place when speaker and listener understand each other. This can be very complicated. Words have different meanings to different people because of their different individual experiences and different cultural backgrounds. Words like love, home, police, and school mean vastly different things to people who live in different parts of town.

Different racial and cultural groups have a language of their own. Perhaps it is more accurate to say a "vocabulary" of their own. This is true of many groups of people—campus groups, prisoners, minority groups, and age groups. Among the poor there is a language that is sometimes called "ghettoese," "the language of the jungle," or what an article in the *New York Times* called the "hidden language of the poor," or the private speech of the ghetto.

The pastor should also be careful that his language has meaning for his counselee. Educated people—pastors, therapists, counselors—tend to communicate in abstractions, often in technical terms. These words have little meaning to one from another culture or one with no formal training. (See Appendix C for a list of terms.)

A pastor whose experience had been primarily with white middle-class people began to work with a group which represented several races; all were poor. He expressed complete frustration. "I can't understand their language," he said. "I don't know what they are talking about." Another pastor leading a group of young blacks was confused by their repeated references to "shooting hooks." Only when he discovered that they were talking about playing hooky did their conversation make sense.

A few examples of how words have different meanings in different parts of town are:

WORD	IN SUBURBIA THE WORD MEANS:	IN POVERTY AREAS THE WORD MAY MEAN:
bread	a food	money
fox	an animal	beautiful girl
cracker	food	white man
hog	an animal	large car
Mother's Day	special Sunday	the day the welfare check arrives
working girl	employed woman	prostitute

"People do seek pastors for help—at least some pastors, who are compassionate, understanding and concerned."

X. Community Resources, Referral, Interprofessional Relationships

Community Resources

One who would minister in poverty areas must know and utilize other community resources.

Anyone who works in poverty areas must be familiar with community resources—both public and private. These would include the welfare offices, old age assistance, aid to families of dependent children, employment services, Goodwill Industries, and any other agencies that provide services for disadvantaged people. (See Appendix E for a list of referral resources.) The Community Council, sometimes called the Council of Social Agencies, has information about all agencies in the community.

There are times when the pastor does not have the time or the skill or the resources to help a person. He does have the responsibility to help the person find those who can help him the most. Some poor people have so many problems (economic, medical, psychological) that several agencies may be needed to meet all of their needs. Many people are not aware that these agencies exist or how to approach them. Others have to be helped to accept such services. They may resist or avoid them for personal or emotional reasons. Some have had unpleasant experiences with agencies in the past and evade or avoid seeking help.

Some agencies are hesitant about working with the clergy, but the majority are willing to cooperate.

A woman, partially paralyzed, was attempting to care for seven children. A 10-year-old did the cooking. Some of the children needed dental care. A 2-year-old was in urgent need of medical care. Medical care was secured for the mother, the children were cared for medically, given vitamin shots; several were placed in foster homes. Financial aid was secured from AFDC. The mother did not know such services were available or how to secure them.

Principles of Referral

A pastor who works with the poor must understand the principles, and develop his skills, of referral.

A knowledge of community resources is the first step. A good referral is based on a full knowledge of the agency. The pastor must understand its purpose and procedures, the fee policy, whether or not there is a waiting list, requirements for admission, or any other matters that will affect the person.

It is helpful if the pastor knows personally the person or persons to whom referral is being made. This isn't always possible, but over a period of time he can develop such relationships.

The person being helped should be prepared in advance for the possibility of referral; he should know the reason for the referral and what to expect. The pastor must recognize there is a "readiness" for referral; at times he may need to continue counseling with the person until such readiness is shown—if the wait does not constitute a risk to the person or to others.

A poor referral may do more harm than good. If an agency is not qualified or cannot accept a person because of legal or residence requirements, it only leads to disappointment and loss of faith in the pastor.

When necessary the pastor can go with the person for his first contact with the agency. This is especially helpful with children, the elderly, the foreign-born, those with a language barrier, etc. He can help with the technicalities of the admitting office, can interpret the person's needs, can occasionally prevent indifference or harsh treatment by the agency. Not the least of the values is to have someone standing by during the experience, which demonstrates concern and alleviates anxiety.

It is important to prepare the agency or the specialist for the referral and to provide them with the kind of information that will enable them to be of most usefulness to the person.

It should be remembered that there can be an element of rejection in all referrals. The pastor may not intend it, or mean it, but the person may feel he is not wanted, that he is being shunted off, that the pastor does not really care.

A pastor should maintain a pastoral relationship throughout the referral. This helps to counteract the feeling mentioned above; but also the agency does not take the place of either church or pastor. They exist to meet certain specific needs. The person still needs the relationship with a pastor. Making a referral does not dismiss a pastoral responsibility.

A pastor called on a woman in a nursing home. Cataracts were forming over her eyes, which eliminated her greatest source of pleasure—reading religious books and magazines. It was suggested that the state department of the blind might help. She agreed. A call to the state department secured a social worker who taught her braille, provided her with a talking book and a braille Bible, taught her to crochet, and arranged for the operation which removed the cataracts. The pastor continued as her pastor.

A pastor was counseling with a young woman who described physical symptoms which may have also been emotional in nature: inability to sleep, lack of appetite, headache, etc. He referred her to a doctor who prescribed rather expensive medicine. He secured funds from an individual who paid for the medication. The pastor continued as the counselor.

Some Problems of the Welfare System

One who works with the poor should understand both the positive and negative reactions to the welfare system.

Many people in poverty areas have had previous experience with the welfare system. Some are economically dependent upon it.

Everyone is grateful for the advances that have come as a result of social legislation. Some welfare workers have a real spirit of compassion and commitment. But there are vast numbers of persons who receive no help and many who receive help but find it very inadequate.

There are also emotional problems that arise out of the welfare system. The welfare system implies inferiority. To qualify, one has to admit he is poor, which is tantamount to admitting he is inferior. It builds dependence. To be dependent on another can destroy one's self-image and lead to resentment and hatred.

The administration of welfare often gives the impression the recipients are mistrusted and are being spied upon; this in turn builds more resentment.

A family with several children all needed medical and dental care. It was arranged so all could be provided by welfare funds that were available. The family refused on the basis they did not accept charity.

When No Referral Is Available

The pastor who works in a poverty area must recognize that there will be times when no referral is available.

In spite of all the developments in recent years—the training of specialists, the multiplication of both public and private services—a pastor will still face situations when no services are available.

Services vary a great deal from community to community. National agencies and local governmental agencies vary greatly in different parts of the country and from one city to another. Many agencies are understaffed and overworked. They, too, have limitations of funds and resources. Many agencies have long waiting lists and, though the services are of a high quality, they may not be available for some time. Some persons' problems are so complex, and in some areas services are so limited, the pastor may find himself with a situation that needs referral but none is available, or none is available at the present time.

On such occasions he should be sure he has exhausted all resources. One criticism social workers make of pastors is that they do not know the resources that are available. They attempt to do things others in the community could do better. All too often a pastor has assumed there was no help when a more thorough search would provide possibilities of help.

If he does make such a search and has no results, then he does the best he can. He is careful not to make mistakes, or get maneuvered into acting as a psychiatrist or as an attorney or some other specialist, when he does not have their specialized training or skills. He functions as a pastor and does the best he can as a pastor.

80

One pastor who has worked extensively with the poor said, "Sometimes I'm a realtor adviser, sometimes a financial adviser, sometimes an employment counselor, sometimes a psychologist, sometimes a social worker; I have to deal with everything, because I can't find anyone else to do it."

The agency may not always agree with a pastor's procedures and methods. A young pastor was working with the staff of a community agency that provided food and clothing for emergency situations. A family came in for emergency food service. They also presented other problems of a personal nature. The pastor suggested they should be given counseling. The workers said, "We don't have time. What they need now is food; counseling they may need but not now. Give them a ride home with their groceries and come back. We've got lots of people to help." He believed they needed marriage counseling, perhaps psychiatric treatment; but there was no one to provide it.

A pastor reported the case of a family that was in real need. The children were hungry. The husband had a job but drank up all his wages. Because he had a job, they were not eligible for financial assistance. The pastor was faced with the fact that the children were still hungry and he had no source of help.

Working with Other Professionals

Pastors who work in a poverty area should expect to have to counsel with other professionals who are working with the poor. This is both a responsibility and an opportunity.

One of the most significant services a pastor can render in a poverty area is to offer counsel and support to other professionals who are also working in the area. This is especially true of young or beginning workers. The problems are so extensive, so vast, that many feel overwhelmed by it all. Most agencies are so understaffed, their funds so limited, and their case loads so large, that they become discouraged, cynical, frustrated—all of which leads to feelings of guilt and inadequacy.

Also, most such persons have a feeling of compassion, but they cannot take their frustrations out on their clients. Hence, they often take them out on each other. This may lead to tense interpersonal relations which are not understood, again producing guilt, hostility, and frustration. A pastor can serve as a mediator, a safety valve for the emotions, or an interpreter of what is taking place. He can help people maintain their sense of mission and their sense of the dignity and worth of man. Thus the pastor helps both the worker and those with whom he works.

A young pastor was working as a pastoral counselor in a social agency. One of the staff of the agency asked the pastor if he would see his daughter, who had become very rebellious and had run away from home.

A clinical psychologist was working with a young pastor with some poor people. The young psychologist asked the pastor if he could discuss his own marital problem with him.

A social worker asked a young pastor to meet with her son who was having problems in school.

A young woman, who as a paraprofessional on the staff of an agency that was located in a poverty area, was heard crying in her office. A pastor knocked on the door and asked if he could help. She said she was overwhelmed by all the suffering. She couldn't help them all, and the other workers didn't seem to care.

The director of an agency told a pastor of his personal frustrations concerning his staff and their relationships. The pastor arranged for a weekend retreat for the entire staff and a group worker who donated his services.

"A pastoral call not only dispels loneliness, it also can be strongly supportive, a source of courage and strength."

XI. Individual Concern and Social Action

Concern for the Community

One who would work with the poor must also be concerned about the conditions in the community and social action as well as individual concerns.

When Walter Rauschenbusch began his ministry on the edge of Hell's Kitchen in New York City in 1886, he had a passion for individual souls. His primary motivation was to save souls and build them up into the "whole faith of God." His biographer said, "He soon found out that conditions were so bad within the city that it was not a safe place for saved souls. Working among the poor and downtrodden, Rauschenbusch began to formulate a program of social action." (Sharpe, *Rauschenbusch,* p. 61.)

Most of the plans and solutions suggested by Walter Rauschenbusch and other pioneers in the social gospel movement are out of date. But the need for social action is still here. All who study the situation of poverty are aware of it. Michael Harrington caught the attention of the presidency. Speaking of the plight of the poor, he said, "They are, in the main, the effects of an environment, not the biographies of unlucky individuals. Because of this, the new poverty is something that cannot be dealt with by first aid. If there is to be a lasting assault on the shame of the other America, it must seek to root out of this society an entire environment and not just relief to individuals." (*The Other America,* p. 18.)

All legitimate influence must be brought to bear on the problems—legislation, education, reform if need be, nondestructive protest. Everyone recognizes that technically, we do not need to have poverty anymore. If we could stab enough consciences, mobilize the resources that are available, poverty could be largely eliminated. Some meaningful steps have been taken. More must be taken.

In the meantime, individuals are hurting. They have needs that must be met, practical problems that should be solved. This is the task of pastoral care.

The very concern that is manifested over poverty in general sometimes diminishes the attention given to the individual poor. An article in the *New York Times* pointed out that in the decade of the sixties it was "poverty itself" that was the object of attention, "rather than the poor." (*Paradox of Poverty in America,* p. 36.)

A young pastor who had been working with the poor said he had to be active in social and community affairs because of the vast numbers of people he saw who were victims of situations that needed to be changed.

A pastor who was located in a poverty area went before the Council of Social Agencies to protest some of their programs which were not effective and to plead for opportunities of cooperation between the pastor and his church and the social workers and their agencies.

The Minister as a Change Agent

Anyone who takes seriously the cause of the poor must improve his skills as an agent of social change.

The two emphases of social action and individual change are often in tension, but they should not be in opposition to each other. In fact, work with individuals who are the victims of poverty should be the primary motivation in working for change within systems.

Anything in society, anything within the systems of our culture that cheapens, degrades, exploits, or destroys personality is evil and should be changed.

Both roles are a part of the historic tradition of the ministry. The minister as shepherd serves as a pastor, working for *individual* change. The minister as prophet serves as an agent of *social* change.

In fact, he who helps individuals change is providing one means of social change. Changing structure without changing individuals is ultimately ineffective. In helping individuals change he gives them strength so they too can become agents of social change.

A pastor was ministering to a lady who was in her 60s. She was two months behind in her rent, the mortgage company was threatening to foreclose. She was very frightened. In addition to his ministry of comfort and reassurance the pastor sought other help and proceeded to take action. He was not sure of her legal rights so he secured legal counsel. He also went before the Greater Housing Opportunity Commission, which interceded in her behalf.

85

A pastor who was concerned about delinquent youth in the poverty neighborhood which surrounded his church appeared before the city council to protest the treatment some had received by authorities and to suggest a plan by which some of these young people could be helped.

Pastoral Care and Social Action—
Both Can Be an Escape

One who works for causes or with individuals must guard against either becoming a form of escape.

It has been pointed out that working with persons on an individual basis can be an escape from facing the harsh realities of the evils in society and the necessity of working for social change. This can be true. Anyone who works for social change must be prepared to accept controversy, face criticism and opposition, and, at times, seeming failure.

The opposite can also be true. One can champion social causes, using this as a means of venting his own hostilities, working off his own guilt and feelings of inadequacy. He can use the "cause" as an escape from the very difficult, at times frustrating, task of helping individuals who are confused, hurting, at times resentful and uncooperative, but who are in deep need of someone with the patience, the sensitivity, the capacity to understand.

The shepherd must beware lest his pastoral work is a means of hiding from being a prophet. The prophet must beware lest his pronouncements and activism are a means of hiding from being a shepherd.

This is a composite description of many pastors, but like other examples given it is based on fact. To some degree it describes all religious workers. Pastor A. is a man who dislikes conflict. He has a deep need to be accepted. He avoids controversial issues. He dislikes the responsibilities and the problems that come with organizations, structures, and groups. He turns to individuals, both because he does have a genuine concern and because he can then justify evading other responsibilities. Pastor B. is a man who feels uncomfortable with individuals. He avoids working with individuals by becoming very active in groups. As one man said of such a pastor, "He makes up projects just to keep active and avoid dealing with persons. Philosophically he is dedicated to care for the individual. Practically, he can't do it."

Pastoral Care Leads to Social Action

The more a pastor sees the victims of injustice, the more he must work for justice.

The test of a culture, a society, a structure, is what it does to people. As was stated earlier, anything that cheapens, degrades, destroys personality is wrong, demonic. The pastor who works with individuals and sees the results in their lives of the pagan, unjust forces in society must work for change so that such tragedies no longer occur. He knows firsthand the pain and suffering that injustice, prejudice, cruelty, and apathy can cause. Out of his concern for his people, the pastor works for a better society. It is this concern that gives him the courage to oppose the demonic forces in society.

The minister, because he does have a pastoral concern, must also be an agent of social change. For some, this may mean political activism; for others, working educationally to provide more knowledge; for still others, it may mean some other approach. The concerned pastor, the faithful shepherd, must also throw the full weight of his influence on the side of justice and change.

A pastor interceded on behalf of a young person who was being arrested because he felt the youth was being mistreated. He found himself subject to possible arrest. He said for the first time he felt fear and anger toward the police, the threat of being jailed; he was the victim of injustice. This, and some other experiences, led to conversations with the juvenile judge, with police authorities, and to some meetings with representatives of the police force with the hope that some understanding and cooperation might be worked out.

A woman sought the help of a pastor because she had been receiving harassing phone calls from a loan company. These had occurred over a long period of time. While he let her vent her feelings, he learned that her husband was in the service overseas. The loan company was threatening to repossess the furniture although over half the debt had been paid and she was only two months behind. The pastor checked with the local Army Recruitment Office. He found that the Soldier and Sailor Relief Act protected servicemen from unethical loan companies. He then arranged for legal consultation and discovered the loan company was subject to suit for some of their actions. He was able to help protect her rights and at the same time help curtail some of the illegal and unfair activities of the loan company, and thus assisted others as well.

"We need much more experience and investigation to answer many of the questions—many more hands need to be enlisted."

XII. The Pastor: His Attitudes and His Identity

Culture Shock

One who would work in a poverty area must be prepared for the possibility of culture shock.

This is not true of those who were raised in a poverty area—for them it is familiar. On the other hand, pastors or theological students who are confronted with poverty on a large scale for the first time should expect a degree of culture shock. The change from their own middle- or upper-class culture to the culture of poverty is just as real and in some ways as extreme as the differences which the missionary or

Peace Corps worker finds in another country. There are different values, different attitudes, different problems, a different vocabulary, different ways of responding. This may take many forms and may have a variety of expressions. Surprise, confusion, feelings of guilt, feelings of inadequacy, and the desire to withdraw are common.

A family of five children, the oldest 7 years of age, were deserted by their parents. After a day and a half they were found by the pastor. The father had deserted first; the mother became discouraged and deserted, leaving them alone. The pastor secured assistance from the police juvenile department, the Department of Welfare, and the United Fund.

A pastor from a middle-class background describes his own feelings when faced for the first time with some of the realities that confronted him in pastoral calling. "I will never forget the first time I went into such a home. It was winter. There was no heat at all in the house. Children were running around naked. The old crippled grandfather sat on the edge of the bed. His retarded wife and his daughter were trying their best to make us comfortable. I sat on the bed next to him. What disgusted me most of all was that the old man didn't even have the energy to swat the flies that crawled all over his face, lips, and eyes. Cockroaches ran like mice across the floor to the kitchen and no one even seemed to notice. I was nauseated."

Pastoral Identity

A pastor who would work in a poverty area should expect difficulty in establishing his own identity with the people and with himself.

People in poverty have various experiences and conflicting concepts of a pastor. (See Appendix D.) They have had limited and often negative experiences with professionals (doctors, lawyers, dentists, welfare workers, etc.). The clergyman who sees himself as a professional man trained in certain skills, such as speaking and counseling, may find the people do not see him in this light at all. They are confused about his identity. The result often is that he then becomes confused about his own identity.

Most graduates of theological seminaries are from middle-class homes. Their concepts of the pastor's role have been influenced by middle-class values and mores. This needs to be altered as they attempt to serve in another cultural group.

The minister who comes from a poor background may also have identity problems. His experiences are an advantage in that they help him understand and relate to the people realistically. But his degrees, in some cases his salary, and his attitudes may be such that the people may feel he has separated himself from them. They may resent his identification with other values. He himself may feel guilty because he has more income, more opportunity, than many of his parishioners.

A woman in a time of difficulty was approached by her pastor, who offered his assistance. She said, "No, I just don't want to talk to you, Pastor. I've been to church all my life and all I got was condemnation."

People often see the pastor's role as something quite practical and materialistic. A pastor calling on a teen-age boy in the hospital said, "I am a pastor. Is there anything I can do for you?" He said, "Yes, bring me a hamburger. I'm hungry."

A High Level of Frustration

One who would work with the poor must develop a capacity to deal with a high level of frustration.

Frustration is built into the situation. There are difficulties of communication that often block a relationship. The pastor will find that familiar methods of counseling are ineffective. He will be confronted by a multiplicity of problems in one situation or with one individual. He will find himself dealing with a different scale of values and different cultural patterns. He may have difficulty establishing his own identity—all of which activates his own feeling of inadequacy. There will be many occasions when he cannot find services in the community to meet specific and practical needs. Just to study the problem in print can be frustrating. The problem is so vast. If the pastor can accept this fact, see it as part of the situation, he can become effective.

A boy from a poor home was not attending school. A pastor calling in the home found he had a badly infected knee which had been injured in the playground. Arrangements for medical care were made. The mother was told that the boy could be treated and get back in school. She asked the boy if he wanted to go to the doctor and to go to school. He didn't want to do either. She refused the help.

A 32-year-old woman was badly beaten by her common-law husband. He blackened her eyes, kicked her in the stomach— injuring her so she needed hospitalization. After this had occurred on several occasions, it was suggested she should seek help about it. She refused, insisting that they could work it out.

There Are Faithful Pastors
Who Work with the Poor

One who would work with the poor should remember there are dedicated pastors—past and present—who have served faithfully and well.

There are men who are serving effectively with people in poverty areas. They are helping people. They are not writing books or articles about it. They probably are not reading much about it either. They are too busy to study or write and are not the kinds of persons who get articles published. They are not asked to appear on programs at conventions, nor do they often get written up in the papers. They usually haven't thought through the psychological and sociological theories of what they are doing. But they do like their people, they have deep religious convictions, they try to help—personally, practically, and spiritually—and they do produce results. People turn to them and trust them, and people are strengthened, sustained, changed, as a result.

A pastor by his presence can offer some support and encouragement. A woman from a very poor home was in a county hospital. She was seriously ill. She said, "I have my faith and I believe in my pastor."

Attitudes Toward the Clergy

A pastor who would work with the poor should expect a variety of attitudes toward the clergy.

The attitude of a counselee toward the counselor is of great importance in determining a counseling relationship. People have a wide variety of attitudes toward the clergy as a group. Each individual's attitudes are shaped and influenced by his previous experiences.

Some of the poor have had no previous relationships with a clergyman and attitudes—good or bad—are almost non-existent.

Some of the poor are members of cult groups or storefront churches. Many of the pastors work through the week and are not available for pastoral services. The poor may not see their pastors as counselors at all.

Some have had unfortunate experiences with clergymen who have taken a patronizing or superior attitude. Such experiences make counseling by a minister very difficult.

Some see the clergyman in terms of a stereotype, as a representative of white middle-class society. Just as the middle class has stereotypes of the poor, so the poor have stereotypes of the middle class. The pastor may be seen in this light.

Some have a good church relationship and a basic trust in the clergy.

At times a pastor will meet both resistance and hostility. A man who had experienced severe and chronic illness said to the pastor who called on him in the county hospital, "I'm not one for you to pray for. If any family has had trouble, we've had it. Just go away."

Some have become disillusioned with religion. A young woman who had experienced a whole series of misfortunes said, "I've just about given up on God."

Some are blunt. They want no part of the church. A pastor called on a man in the county hospital. He said, "I am Pastor _____. Is there anything I can do for you?" The man replied, "No."

Others express a real need for a ministry and great gratitude for its value. One woman in time of deep trouble asked for a pastor because she needed "some assurances." A family after a period of trouble and illness expressed appreciation for their pastor's presence. They said it "made them feel they were not alone after all."

Some Attitudes and Procedures to Avoid

One who would minister in poverty areas must avoid certain attitudes and procedures.

We are influenced by the attitudes others take toward us. This is especially true of people with authority or influence. The attitudes of a preacher, doctor, teacher determine the response they receive from their parishioner, patient, and pupil, as much as does their knowledge or skill. This is particularly true with the poor who have been subjected to so much mistreatment. There are some attitudes which must be carefully avoided if one is to be accepted by them. All we can do is list them. They need no explanation.

One must avoid any expression of superiority or any implication that they are inferior. This is not only unkind, it is untrue. They must be seen as equals. Maybe not equals in circumstances, but equals in the sight of God.

⁓One must avoid the "lady bountiful" attitude at all costs. It can only result in resentment.

⁓One should avoid any sentimentality. The poor are very realistic.

⁓One should avoid piety. As one young black said of his pastor, "Man, you just don't feel comfortable talking to him in your own language."

⁓One should avoid any patronizing attitude, or self-righteousness—"How good I am to be helping you poor people."

⁓One must avoid forcing his value system on others. That is discussed elsewhere in these pages. The pastor has his, the poor have theirs. One is just as valid as the other.

⁓One may need to avoid any formal, structured, professional attitudes. The poor have often been conditioned against professionals who have patronized or exploited them.

A young pastor from a white middle-class background describes how he struggled with his feelings as he approached his first assignment in a multiracial, poor community. "As I was driving to my first meeting with the people, I could not help but think, 'How should I present myself to these people?' I had never worked in a situation with members of another race or with people who were poor. I had grown up with many prejudices which I now despised. Yet, the more I thought about it, the more the old myths which rise up out of prejudice came back to haunt me. Would they hate me because I am white? Would they resent me because of the car I drive? Should I go in assuming I had knowledge which they did not? If the assumption was correct, should I let them know right off that I had some authority I could kindly allow them to use? How silly! So, I quickly raised more questions of strategy which I thought would be more acceptable to them. Shouldn't I approach them as the humble, suffering servant? Shouldn't I come on like the completely liberated white man, free from all racial or class prejudice and indignant because of the injustices visited upon minorities and the poor?"

How this pastor and every pastor resolves such questions to a large extent determines his effectiveness in ministering to the poor. It is not only the attitudes he assumes that are important. It is also the ones he avoids.

Attitudes Necessary to Work in the Poverty Area

One who would minister to persons in poverty areas must cultivate and develop certain attitudes himself.

There are certain attitudes that are necessary for the pastor to develop if he is to be an effective counselor with any group or any person. The following attitudes include nothing that is a unique requirement for working in a poverty area. We include them because they are basically so important in any discussion of pastoral care, and also because the problems of the poor are so acute that they are particularly important in working with them.

Humility. One must be conscious of his own limitations. Any attitude of arrogance or superiority will be self-defeating.

Patience. Results are small and may come slowly. Obstacles are enormous. One must be satisfied with small gains.

Acceptance. Some of the poor, especially the young, resent the efforts of any counselors. The alienation that the poor person may feel toward others quite naturally also includes the counselor. The counselor should not be surprised or resentful of it. The counselor must accept the person as he is, with his resistance and his resentment, if he is to help.

Imagination and empathy. One must develop the capacity to put himself in another's place and to feel as he feels. This is never completely possible. Ezekiel said of the captives by the river Chebar, "I sat where they sat." No one can do this completely. Some even say it is impossible for one who has never known poverty firsthand to empathize with the poor. We agree, it is difficult—not impossible.

Understanding. No one fully understands another, and when one is from a different cultural group it is even more difficult. However, he can try, and the degree that one tries will greatly influence the effectiveness of his counseling. If a person feels that the pastor is sincerely trying to understand, this in itself is helpful.

Optimism. This paragraph must be closely joined with the next. One must be optimistic. This optimism must be realistically related to the situation, but one must expect some results to take place. He must feel that some possibilities for growth are present. In most cases they are. Optimism may take years of experience to develop, and admittedly requires a large amount of faith and hope, but it is all-important.

Realism. The optimism must be realistic. The pastor must face facts and recognize the complexity and extent of a situation. Poor people have little respect for the "do-gooder" who is superficially or sentimentally optimistic, who can be easily conned, who is unaware of the realities of the situation.

Appreciation and respect. One in a middle-class culture should appreciate that the traditional manner of speech, dress, activities, moral practices, and beliefs, which other groups have developed are their way of meeting the tasks of life and have real value for them. Stating it negatively, one should not look down on another culture or the people in it.

Commitment. Bagdikian says, "It takes a special kind of person and a serious commitment" to work with the poor. This is true.

The above attitudes are difficult anywhere but especially in a poverty area. One young pastor who had had considerable experience of a great deal of deprivation and who has carried on a rather extensive pastoral responsibility said, "Sometimes the strain is just incredible. The emotional strain can get unbearable." In fact, he and a group of other pastors met regularly to work through some of their own attitudes.

People do respond to a minister in time of difficulty. A pastor called on a woman who had experienced much difficulty and considerable pain. His ministry was primarily one of support and reassurance. She said to him, "You have been very helpful. It has made this whole thing much easier."

Appendix A. Selected References of Biblical Teachings on the Poor and Social Welfare Concerns

The Law

The codes of law found in the Old Testament included a real spirit of compassion and concern, coupled with specific practical instructions for dealing with persons who needed help.

Exodus 23:10-11
(The poor)

The law expressed real humanitarian concern and provided a means for providing for the poor.

"For six years you shall sow your land and gather in its yield; but the seventh year you shall let it rest and lie fallow, that the poor of your people may eat."

Leviticus 19:9-10; 23:22
(The poor, travelers, and strangers)

Corners of the field are to be left unharvested; some of the grapes on the vine and those fallen to the ground are to be left for the poor and sojourners.

Leviticus 25:3-6
(The poor, slaves, and traveler)

"Six years you shall sow your field, and six years you shall prune your vineyard, and gather in its fruits; but in the seventh year there shall be a sabbath of solemn rest for the land, a sabbath to the Lord. . . . The sabbath of the land shall provide food for you, for yourself, and for your male and female slaves and for your hired servant and the sojourner who lives with you." The uses are charitable but the purpose is theological. The land itself shall "observe the sabbath."

"And you shall not strip your vineyard bare, neither shall you gather the fallen grapes of your vineyard; you shall leave them for the poor and for the sojourner: I am the Lord your God."

Leviticus 25:35-39
(Loans for the poor)

Loans to the poor are to be without interest. "And if your brother becomes poor, and cannot maintain himself with you, you shall maintain him. . . . Take no interest from him or increase."

They could accept him as a hired servant but not as a slave.

Deuteronomy 14:28-29
(The poverty of travelers, orphans, and widows)

Every third year the tithe to be stored for relief of poverty, provision for traveler, orphan, and widow.

Deuteronomy 15:7-8
(The poor)

"If there is among you a poor man, . . . you shall open your hand to him, and lend him sufficient for his need." They were not only to provide for his physical need but to see him as a brother.

Deuteronomy 15:9-11
(The poor)

To give to the "poor brother" was a requirement, but more than this the attitudes by which it was done were important. "You shall give to him freely, and your heart shall not be grudging when you give to him; because for this the Lord your God will bless you in all your work. . . . For the poor will never cease out of the land, therefore I command you, You shall open wide your hand to your brother, to the needy and to the poor, in the land."

99

Deuteronomy 23:15 (Slaves)	Runaway slaves are to be given refuge. This is contrary to all practices of that day.
Deuteronomy 23:24-25 (Travelers)	Grain and fruit in the fields to be available to travelers, but the privilege was not to be abused.
Deuteronomy 24:14-15 (Servants, the poor)	Do not oppress a servant, because God is especially concerned for the poor and will count it as a sin against the master.
Deuteronomy 24:19-22 (Traverlers, orphans, and widows)	Some products to be left in fields and vineyards for the needy to glean.
Ruth 2	Ruth gleaning in fields in accordance with the law requiring some produce to be left for the poor.

The Prophets

The prophets denounced those who oppressed the poor and demanded that people adhere to the requirements of the law. Amos, Isaiah, Micah, and others spoke heroically against oppressors. The prophets implied that God "remembers," or is mindful of, the poor. He cares for them in a special way and desires they should have access to material needs.

Isaiah 1:17 (Injustice, orphans, and widows)	Isaiah urged the people to "learn to do good; seek justice, correct oppression; defend the fatherless, plead for the widow." There were no provisions for the unfortunate except what the people provided. With Isaiah it was a religious obligation.
Isaiah 11:4 (The poor)	The poor will receive special consideration from God: "With righteous-

ness he shall judge the poor, and decide with equity for the meek."

Isaiah 17:5,6
(The poor and the limitations of provisions for them)

Points out that the law requiring gleanings to be left in fields often provided scanty fare. All that may be left is "two or three berries in the top of the highest bough, four or five on the branches of a fruit tree."

Isaiah 41:17
(God's concern for poor)

"When the poor and needy seek water, and there is none, and their tongue is parched with thirst, I the Lord will answer them, I the God of Israel will not forsake them."

Isaiah 61:1
(The unfortunate, the discouraged, and prisoners)

The prophetic call was "to bring good tidings to the afflicted, . . . to bind up the brokenhearted, to proclaim liberty to the captives, and the opening of the prison to those who are bound."

Ezekiel 18:12; 22:29
(Oppression of poor condemned)

To oppress the poor is equated with robbery. A nation is condemned if it oppresses the poor and needy.

Amos 4:1; 5:12
(Against oppression of the poor)

Amos spoke repeated warnings against those who "oppress the poor, crush the needy," for their own pleasure, or those who "turn aside the needy in the gate."

Wisdom Literature

The wisdom literature contains frequent references to the poor and unfortunate. Those who oppressed the poor were condemned, whereas God himself was seen as having a special concern for the poor.

Psalms 9:18
(The poor)

God is revealed as one who is concerned for the poor.

"For the needy shall not always be forgotten, and the hope of the poor shall not perish for ever."

Psalms 41:1
(The poor)

Concern for the poor is pleasing to God; "Blessed is he who considers the poor!"

Psalms 72:12-14
(The poor and needy)

God has a special concern for the poor. "He has pity on the weak and the needy, and saves the lives of the needy."

Proverbs 13:8, 23;
14:20, 21
(The poor)

The book of Proverbs expresses concern for the poor; it discusses their problems and speaks with favor of those who show kindness. "Happy is he who is kind to the poor."

Proverbs 19:17; 21:13
(The poor)

Implies that to help the poor is to render service to God: "He who is kind to the poor lends to the Lord." Furthermore, not to do so may create problems: "He who closes his ear to the cry of the poor will himself cry out and not be heard."

Proverbs 22:9; 28:27
(The poor)

One who "shares his bread with the poor" will be blessed. "He who gives to the poor will not want."

Proverbs 31:9
(Rights of the poor)

Rights of the poor to be upheld: "Open your mouth, judge righteously, maintain the rights of the poor and needy."

Proverbs 31:20
(Charity, the poor)

A good woman is industrious, provides food for the household and "opens her hand to the poor, and reaches out her hands to the needy."

102

The Gospels

The Gospels picture one who demonstrated unlimited love and compassion and who demands the same of his followers.

Luke 4:18-19
(The poor, oppressed, and captives)

Jesus' ministry was begun by quoting from Isaiah, "The Spirit of the Lord is upon me, because he has anointed me to preach good news to the poor, . . . to proclaim release to the captives, and recovering of sight to the blind, to set at liberty those who are oppressed."

Matthew 6:20; Mark 10: 21; Luke 12:33; 18:22
(Give to poor to have treasures in heaven)

When one inquired what he must do to inherit eternal life, he was told to sell what he had, give to the poor, and follow Christ.

Luke 10:30-37
(True neighborliness)

The Good Samaritan—perhaps the most influential story for good ever told, emphasizes anyone in need is one's neighbor. After the Samaritan's kindness had been recognized, Jesus said, "Go and do likewise."

Luke 14:12-14
(Consideration of poor, crippled—all who cannot repay)

The parable of the feast urged to invite "the poor, the maimed, the lame, the blind, and you will be blessed, because they cannot repay you."

Matthew 25:31-46
(The hungry, thirsty, naked, sick, strangers, prisoners)

Righteous separated from unrighteous on basis of whether they fed the hungry, clothed the naked, welcomed strangers, visited the sick and imprisoned. Complete identification "as you did it to one of the least of these my brethren, you did it to me."

Acts and Epistles

The early church as described in the book of Acts and the early letters continued this spirit of compassion and concern.

Acts 4:34-35
(The needy)

They cared for their own even at point of great sacrifice, "There was not a needy person among them, for as many as were possessors of lands or houses sold them, and brought the proceeds . . . and laid it at the apostles' feet; and distribution was made to each as any had need."

Acts 6:1-6

First church officials appointed to minister to needs of people.

Galatians 2:10
(The poor)

Paul ministered to poor as part of his apostolic duties. "They would have us remember the poor, which very thing I was eager to do."

James 1:27
(Widows, orphans, and the afflicted)

Pure religion is defined as rendering service to those in need and keeping oneself unspotted from the world.

James 2:1-7
(The poor in the synagogue)

James condemns the church for showing partiality and special attention to the rich and ignoring the poor.

I John 3:17-18
(Those in need)

Love for God manifested in those who live deeds of love. "But if any one has the world's goods and sees his brother in need, . . . how does God's love abide in him? Little children, let us not love in word or speech but in deed and truth."

Appendix B. Men of Compassion

The church has never been without witnesses to its concern for the poor. For centuries, it was the primary agency that offered specific and practical help to the hungry, the homeless, the orphaned, and the unfortunate.

There have been some outstanding persons whose heroic and sacrificial efforts are an inspiration to men in all times and places. A knowledge of their efforts is a challenge to wider service.

Francesco Bernardone (1182-1226), better known as St. Francis of Assisi, lived in the period known as the Dark Ages. He was born into a wealthy family but became a friend of the poor. He took the very clothes off his back and gave them to a beggar. He assumed voluntary poverty as an act of obedience to Christ. His efforts and his spirit shed the first light of the Dark Ages.

August Francke (1663-1727) was a pastor in the village of Glauchau. He had a concern for the poor—especially the children. When poor children came to his parsonage seeking bread, he took them into his study and questioned them about the catechism. He was so concerned that he went without supper to secure funds to send poor children to school. In 1694, when he discovered that some did not use the money to go to school, he established his own school for the poor. This "ragged" school was a pioneer experiment in the field of education. He also founded several orphanages and a program of free meals for poor university students, who in turn taught in his school.

William Law (1686-1761) is perhaps best known as the author of the devotional classic, *A Serious Call to a Devout and Holy Life*. On receiving a gift of one thousand pounds from an unidentified contributor, he used it to establish a school for fourteen poor children. This began a widespread, often naïve, but extremely generous ministry to the poor of London's extensive slum areas. In the midst of these activities he both maintained and wrote about the devotional life.

John Wesley (1703-1791), founder of the Methodist Church, an evangelist who said the whole world was his parish, was very conscious of the physical and personal needs of people. His messages were directed toward the downtrodden. One biographer said, "He had a genius for finding the poor and neglected." He established a house of mercy for poor and destitute widows, a dispensary for the distribution of medication to the poor, a book room for providing cheap but approved literature, a bank for savings and for providing relief to the needy.

Robert Raikes (1735-1811) was not a clergyman but a businessman who was concerned about the poor children of the town of Gloucester. There were no child labor laws and no public schools. Since the children worked all week and were cut adrift on Sundays, he got a group together and started a Sunday school. For some time, the Sunday school movement was not popular with many people in the established churches because it was considered a program for the poor.

William Booth (1829-1912) was raised in poverty. He was bound for several years as an apprentice when he was only thirteen years old. Knowing poverty by personal experience, he gave himself to the people of the slums of London where it was said, "All the sorrows of the world knocked on his door." It was said of Booth: "He realized the sorrows of others in a surpassing degree: in their affliction he was afflicted; in their hunger he was hungered; in their poverty he was distressed; with their diseases he was stricken; by their strifes he was beaten and tormented; in their wanderings his own great spirit wandered through the earth." Out of his deep concern for the poor the Salvation Army came into being.

Walter Rauschenbusch (1861-1918) began his ministry at the turn of the century in a little Baptist church on the edge of Hell's Kitchen in New York City. It was a tough, crowded, difficult neighborhood. He ministered to a congregation of tenement dwellers most of whom, he said, were "out of shoes, out of jobs, out of hope." It was here, through his ministry, he hoped to make "a little spot in this world a better place to live in." It was said of him, "He could not resist the cry of the needy."

He soon discovered that trying to save individual souls was not enough. One must change the conditions that destroyed the souls.

As a result, he began to express some of his convictions in writing, which became the spearhead of the social gospel movement. "Dear Friends," he wrote, "there is a social question. No one can doubt it, in whose ears are ringing the wails of the mangled and crushed, who are borne along on the torment of life. Woe to the man who stands afar off and says, 'Peace, peace,' when there is no peace. . . . Let us take heed lest we too bow to that which is, and refuse allegiance to that which ought to be." (Sharpe; *Rauschenbusch*, p. 61.)

Washington Gladden (1836-1918), preacher, social prophet, hymn writer, wrote a book in 1898 called *The Christian Pastor*. The concluding chapter was entitled "The Care of the Poor." His first sentence was, "It might almost be said that the Christian Church was organized for the care of the poor." He was very critical of the church of his day because in its affluence it was neglecting the poor. "The deepest need of these poor," he said, "is manliness and self-respect. This need will not be supplied by a lavish or careless bestowment of alms; a judicious withholding of material aid will often be more charitable to them than any amount of giving. The thing to be first considered in their case is the interest of character. Whatever will encourage them to help themselves is true charity; whatever tends to lighten their feeling of responsibility and to weaken their self-reliance is mistaken kindness. . . . It is easy to send a ton of coal or a barrel of flour; it is not easy to arouse the dormant will or to quicken the sense of honor. . . . To recognize the fact that Christ came to save these people, not primarily from suffering, but from sin and weakness and moral degradation—to make the primary condition of successful ministry to their deepest need. A genuine friendship is the best medicine for them—a friendship which conveys to them, by sympathy and inspiration, the saving vigor of the very life of Christ. Their primary need is a spiritual need." (*The Christian Pastor* [Scribners, 1896], p. 454.)

Graham Taylor (1851-1938), like most men of his day, began his ministry with a passion for individual souls. His church in Hartford seated twelve hundred, but fewer than fifty people were in attendance. Finding that people did not come to church, he went to the people. "He visited the jails and the state prison and talked to men through cell bars. He went from house to house, office to office, and tenement to tenement, meeting men and women where they worked and lived." The people began to come to church in great numbers. He in turn learned how they lived. He began to make statements considered rather extreme in those days. "You can't save the souls of the children down in Charles Street," he said, "without taking notice of the Charles Street muck in which they live."

He moved to Chicago and taught in a seminary. He was one of the first to apply sociological findings to the work of the church. In his teaching and his activity he never lost sight of the needs of the individual. His biography includes case after case of people whom he helped. In order to render a wider service he established Chicago Commons, a social settlement house, and worked there in addition to his teaching and training of theological students.

There are many other names that could be added. These are simply a few who are illustrative of the fact that the Christian church has always had some men who had a deep feeling of compassion and who expressed it in very practical and specific ways. The motivation which challenged and sustained them must be related to the personal and social needs of today.

Appendix C. Communication: The "Hidden Language of the Poor"

The following terms are illustrative of some of the expressions that have different meanings in different cultural groups. They are then defined in general terms. It should be pointed out that such jargon varies with each subculture; it varies from city to city, and changes very rapidly. These terms have been collected from a number of sources and represent only a small percentage of such expressions that could have been included.

Ace—to do very well.
Aunt Sally—female equivalent of "Uncle Tom."
Backdoor artist—an addict who cheats other addicts.
Bad news—an uncomfortable or dangerous situation.
Bad vibes—bad vibrations, meaning a situation or group is unsympathetic or unfriendly.
Bag—an area of interest, reflecting one's personality, problem.
Barge—A big car, a Cadillac.
Bastille—jail.
Big Juice—a big-time white racketeer, usually getting police protection.
Black—the term preferred over Negro, colored, or any other term for black people.
Bloody Mary—a mean teacher.
Blow—what a person says, his message; or to split, or leave.
Blow one's cool—to allow oneself to become unduly excited.
Bomb—to mess something up, to fail.
Bread—money.
Brother—usually, though not always, another black person.
Buckwheat—a nickname for a friend.
Bug—to bother.
Bug out—to drop out, to leave, to quit.
Bulldogger—a female homosexual who assumes a male role.
Bum-beefed—framed by the police.
Burn—to improvise well in music, or experience; to discipline or punish.
Burner—the top in his field.

Burnt—stolen.

Bust—an arrest.

Bust-heads—smart children.

Butch—a female homosexual who assumes a male role.

Butt out—go away!

Caddy—a patronizing teacher.

Capping—trying to outdo other children or youths in trading insults, usually deprecating the other family.

Chuck—a white man.

Clean—well dressed, excellently attired, same as dap.

Cleaned out—whipped, beaten.

Clear field—good chance to date girls.

Clyde Beatty—a strict teacher.

Cool—something attractive, desirable, highly acceptable.

Cool cat—a person with whom there is immediate rapport.

Cool head—a person who treats people well.

Cool it—"Stop what you are doing!"; keep under control.

Cool jerk—one who thinks he knows what is going on but really does not.

Cop a plea—to plead guilty or admit to a fault; to inform; to back out of a situation.

Cover—protection from police through bribery or other arrangements.

Crack up—to smile, or laugh.

Cracker—a white man, a red-neck.

Creep—a strange person.

Crib—house, home.

Cub scouts—amateurs, people without experience.

Cut out—to leave a place.

Dap—impeccably attired.

Deep in the mud—embarrassed.

Devil—a Caucasian.

Dig—to understand.

Dip—a pickpocket.

Do a grand—to do well.

Dog—an unattractive girl.

Dog food—bribes for police, judges, etc.

Doss—an attractive girl.

Dude—a male.

Eagle—aggressive action, the opposite of chicken.

Fade away—go away.

Fem—a female homosexual who assumes the feminine role.

Fence—a place where stolen goods are bought and sold.

Fin—five dollars.

Five finger discount—a theft.

Fix the meter—to cheat in class.

Flake—one who does strange things; one who is not too bright.

Fleas—nice children; or unimportant persons.

Fox—beautiful girl or female.

Freak out—lose control.

Get sapped—to get in a bad deal; to get in an accident.

Gig—a party; a job.

Gold is my color—pay me in advance.

Golden butterfly—a nice teacher.

Green—money.

Grind on—to dance very close to one's partner.

Groove, groovy—excellent, smooth, wonderful; a good thing.

Handkerchief head—an "Uncle Tom."

Hang loose—to stay calm under pressure.

Hang someone up—to cause annoyance to another person; to inconvenience him; to make him wait.

Hang-up—problem or difficulty.

Happening—event.

Hip—informed on current events.

Hipped to it—to be in the know; to be modern.

Hog—any large automobile.

Hub—the office of a school.

Hummer—a nothing person or event.

Hung up—to be obsessed with something.

Jive—an unreliable person; a persuasive talker.

Keep the shoelaces tied—to control things.

Keep your cool—to stay calm.

Lame—a person who is not in tune with the important events of the world; a boring character; a socially backward person.

Little red wagon—social problem, bag.

Long drive—defying a teacher or other authority.

Low rent—a girl with low moral standards.

Lurken (Lurking)—joyride.

Main man—a woman's boyfriend.

Member—an Afro-American soul brother.

Miss Ann—Caucasian or Negro woman; also called Aunt Sally. An ingratiating woman, one who flatters people in order to get on in the world.

Mister Charlie—Caucasian, or the "boss man."

Mother's Day—the day when the welfare check arrives.

Nitty gritty—the basic essence or heart of the matter.

Now—a general term for anything contemporary, regarded as worthy of notice; that is, there can be a *now* person, a *now* style of dress, etc.

Old lady—a girl friend.

Oreo-cookie—a person who is black but lives and thinks like a white.

Out-of-sight—beyond comparison; good looking; out-of-this-world.

Pay one's dues—accept discipline.

Pepper belly—a Latin-(Mexican-) American.

Pig—a police officer.

Playing the dozens—same as capping; trading insults, usually in rhyme.

Put in cold storage—punish.

Rabbits—timid children or persons.

Rap—same as blow; a person's message; to converse with someone about nothing in particular.

Rat—to plead guilty; to admit; to inform.

Rib—girl, woman.

Rip off—to take or steal.

Scoot—a motorcycle, the type often used by the Hell's Angels.

Scramble—gang up on someone.

Scratch—money.

Send hotcakes—pass notes.

Set—a close gathering, usually good.

Shoot down with grease—to play dirty tricks.

Shooting hooks—playing hooky.

Slave—a job.

Smoking—to be angry.

Some tired paths—poor lessons.

Soul—term used to describe people—as soul brother, a culture—as the Afro-American, or things—food; black term for courage, sensibility, style, etc. The spiritual bond felt by blacks for each other.

Soul brother—used by one black to another whether or not they are acquainted.

Soul food—good fresh food which has been neither canned nor frozen; often refers to pork, greens, black-eyed peas, and cornbread.

Soul language—idioms and slang used by blacks between themselves.

Soul power—the strength shown by minority groups, especially blacks, in their forms of protest and civil disobedience. The bond of feeling which can be used constructively to improve economic conditions.

Soul session—a gathering of black people; a dance; a discussion; or an entertainment of some kind.

Soul sister—any female black. Used to describe a black in the same situation as oneself. She may be a friend, or acquaintance, or even a stranger.

Soul sound—good music; harmony which appeals to blacks.

Soul survivors—a group of white singers whose music appeals to blacks.

Soul talk—meaningful conversation between blacks.

Special pine top—a nice teacher.

Square—same as lame; socially backward.

Stalled—to be puzzled, confused.

Stay low—to hide.

Stone fox—an attractive girl.

Strung out—to be in love.

Stud—a boy.

Tack head—a patronizing teacher.

Tadpoles—classmates in ghetto school.

That's clean—attractive.

The bull—the police (used by Mexican-Americans and blacks).

The man—the police, an employer, or boss.

Thing—an activity which one enjoys doing, regardless of whether other people approve.

Threads—clothes.

T.L.C.—tender loving care.

Tomcat—a sly, sometimes ruthless leader, usually used in reference to students.

Too much—very nice.

Tree—a policeman who accepts bribes.

Trilly along—to join the group.

Umbrella—protection from police through bribery or other arrangements.

Uncle Tom—a black who yields to white pressures, etc.

Unzip the teacher—make a teacher back down.

Uptight—tense.

Vulliene—a mean teacher.

Walk cool—to take life easily.

Working girl—a prostitute.

Zap—destroy, take sudden action.

Appendix D.   Comparison and Contrast of Pastoral Care in Suburbia and in Poverty Areas

The question is frequently asked, Are there any differences in pastoral care in the traditional Protestant churches in suburbia and a church located in a poverty area? The following chart emphasizes some of these differences. It is recognized that they are not always present, nor are they insurmountable. The left-hand column indicates the situation that is characteristic of suburbia. The right-hand column represents poverty areas.

Suburbia	*Poverty*
The pastor's role is fairly well understood and usually is accepted by the group with which he works. (He may have trouble establishing his own identity as a pastor, but it is not complicated by different concepts of the people as may be true in a poverty area.)	May have difficulty establishing his identity as a pastor. Role concepts are often confused and unclear.
No problem of culture shock—of being overwhelmed by the environment.	Possibility of real culture shock if the pastor is unfamiliar with the problems of the poor.
Pastor has usually experienced the same type of environment as his parishioners.	Pastor from middle or upper class who works with the poor is dealing with people whose lives are influenced by the "culture of poverty."
Pastor in suburbia represents a church which is generally ac-	Pastor in poverty area represents a church some people feel

Suburbia	Poverty
cepted as part of the community. It may be criticized by the young, but generally is considered good.	has deserted them, patronized them, ignored them.
Social or emotional problems are similar to his own and those he is used to.	The pastor may be emotionally overwhelmed by the vastness and extent of the social and economic problems that are present.
A fairly high percentage of people maintain at least nominal affiliation with the church. It may not be active; it may not represent any deep commitment, but they have some contact.	Only a small percentage of the poor maintain any affiliation with the church.
Theological training has prepared him to understand this cultural group.	Theological training given almost no understanding of this cultural group.
Pastoral care courses and literature make strong emphasis on the problems of the middle class.	Pastoral care courses and literature make few references to problems of this cultural group.
Pastoral care methods drawn from psychotherapy are effective in middle-class culture.	Pastoral care methods often do not apply to the culture of poverty.
No problem of communication. Pastor and parishioners speak the same language.	Communication can be very difficult. The poor and minority groups often have a vocabulary of their own.
People (usually) understand and accept the idea of counseling.	People may not understand and often do not accept the concept of counseling.

Suburbia	Poverty
People have had previous wholesome, positive contacts with the helping professions—doctors, dentists, etc. This prepares them for counseling.	People have had only limited contacts with helping professions; some have had none at all or often negative experiences. Creates negative attitudes toward counseling.
Usually does counseling with members of his own race. No racial barriers or suspicion.	Often does counseling with members of other races or minority groups and faces barriers of suspicion and hostiilty.
People have had past experiences of success and satisfaction on which to build.	People have had very limited, if any, experiences of success and therefore may lack motivation to try.
Counseling can be growth-oriented, lending itself to verbalization.	Counseling often must be action-oriented, seeking specific solutions.
People are more talk-oriented; situations can be verbalized.	People less talk-oriented, prefer advice and guidance.
Problems are centered around emotion and feeling. Practical and economic problems not often taken to pastor.	People have immediate, practical, economic problems having to do with food, jobs, clothing, bail, etc.
Pastor usually has a study or an office where counseling can take place in quiet, undisturbed atmosphere.	Some churches have offices, many do not. Counseling must be done everywhere.
A pastoral call in the home can often find a person available for uninterrupted conversation.	A call in the home rarely provides opportunity for quiet discussion. Rooms are small, many people may be present, children may be coming and going.

Suburbia	**Poverty**
Pastor can concentrate on personal and emotional problems.	Economic problems often so pressing that one cannot center on feelings or psychological problems until economic ones are relieved.
People may be dissatisfied with housing—but pastor seldom deals with housing as such.	Housing may be central problem, especially with elderly.
The psychological problems of life space are not often central.	The psychological results of inadequate life space are very common.
People have not been subject to indignities, police brutality, patronizing, etc.	People have been subject to so many frustrations so long that much deep-rooted resentment emerges.
Can usually be motivated to work toward delayed or long-range goals.	Because he only knows his present situation it is difficult for a poor person to be motivated for anything other than immediate or short-term goals.
The pastor's motives and intentions not frequently questioned.	Pastor's motives and intentions may be subject to considerable question and testing.
May make referral to specialists, usually medical and psychiatric.	Often need referral to welfare agencies, Salvation Army, etc.
Questions of funds for referral not a major item. (There are many obvious exceptions.)	Funds for fees almost always a factor.
People have not been dependent on welfare and social agencies for support,	People subjected to the dependency feelings generated by the welfare system, often to indig-

Suburbia	Poverty
	nities, with all the emotional accompaniments of such experiences.
Only occasionally need referral for legal services. (They may need and use legal services but they do not come to the pastor with these problems.)	Often need legal counsel and advice.
Seldom refer for the necessities of life: food, clothing, etc.	Frequently need assistance in area of bare necessities of life.

Appendix E.   Referral Resources

The following is a list of most of the referral resources related to poverty that are available to a pastor, with their preferred training and a summary of the services they offer.

Each pastor needs to develop his own working list of persons and agencies that are available in his community for help. This should include the names, addresses, and phone numbers, as well as such matters as hours, fee policy, etc. In a larger community, the Council of Social Agencies (sometimes called the Community Council) or the United Fund (Community Chest) has such a list. In a rural community, the county welfare office can usually provide such information. A pastor who has been in the community for some time can often provide information about the policies and attitudes of other professionals and the agencies in the community.

Chaplain, Institutional: B.D. or M.Div. and special clinical training in pastoral care.

Member of staff of state hospitals, general hospitals, penal and correctional institutions, homes for older people, schools for retarded, etc.

Chaplain, Military: B.D. or M.Div. and pastoral experience; special training by military.

Serves as pastor in various branches of armed forces.

Child Welfare Worker: Social work training.

Specializes in alleviation of child welfare problems. Attempts to prevent exploitation of minors. Helps physically handicapped children. Finds foster homes and other institutional care. Serves on staff of county and state welfare departments.

Community Action Agency Worker (OEO): Some are trained in social work; the majority are not. Many represent minority groups and have experienced problems of discrimination and poverty firsthand.

Works in all kinds of areas—securing jobs, emergency food and medical service, etc.

Community Mental Health Center

Provides multiple services in the areas of mental health and retardation. Fees adjusted to ability to pay.

Employment Worker: No common standard of training.

Assists people in finding employment. Interviews applicants for jobs; utilizes vocational testing, counseling, etc. Serves on staff of U.S. Employment Service or some private agencies.

Family Counselor: Many combinations of training. Usually includes psychological, sociological, and social work, with emphasis on family life.

Helps solve problems affecting family—family tension, divorce, care of children, etc. Usually refers psychiatric problems to other specialists. Serves on staff of Family Service Association; some in private practice.

Guidance Worker: Master's in educational psychology preferred minimum.

Helps with academic and learning problems; specializes in educational and vocational planning. Assists with emotional problems. On staff of large school systems; in smaller schools, also does teaching.

Mission Worker: Religious training, no minimum standard.

Works with transients, lower socioeconomic groups. Combines religious and social work approach. Serves on staff of city missions, rescue missions, etc.

Parole Officer: Social work training preferred; many do not have it.

Works with delinquents and criminals who are on parole from corrective institutions; attempts to help with rehabilitation.

Probation Officer: Social work training preferred; many do not have it.

Responsible for delinquents who are on probation; takes case histories, counsels; works with courts.

Psychiatric Social Worker: Master's in social work, minimum.

Does case work with persons suffering from nervous or emotional problems. Usually on staff of hospital or institution.

Psychiatrist: M.D. and psychiatric training.

Specializes in treatment of nervous and emotional diseases. Serves on staff of hospitals, child guidance clinics, or in private practice.

Public Health Nurse: Nurses' training.

Available for service in public health department; also in homes, with elderly, maternity care, etc. On staff of Department of Public Health.

Red Cross Worker: Social work training preferred, although not all have it.

Provides communication for servicemen in need of leave, etc. Serves in disaster areas. Home Service Department does some casework counseling.

Rehabilitation Offices

Counsels adults with problems of vocational choice and training.

Salvation Army Worker: Special training by Salvation Army.

Carries on variety of services; works with transients, unwed mothers; finds employment; does religious welfare work, etc. Salvation Army offices are found almost everywhere.

School Psychologist: M.A., sometimes Ph.D. in educational psychology.

Specializes in testing and counseling, or academic problems and vocational choice. Also deals with mild psychiatric problems. On staff of larger school systems.

Social Worker: Master's in social work.

Covers many fields; works to alleviate and prevent social problems by providing counseling, monetary grants, vocational and avocational opportunities. Especially well-acquainted with community resources. Serves on staff of private, religious, state, federal, and county agencies.

Travelers Aid Worker: Social work training preferred; not a requirement.

Assists in solving problems due to travel; helps children traveling alone; helps people who are lost. Aids travelers in need of financial assistance. Helps transients find their destination.

Visiting Teacher: A.B., teaching experience, plus social work training.

Assists children who find difficulty in adapting to school life. Counsels with children and their parents who need individual help.

Arranges for medical, psychiatric, and other services when indicated.

Vocational Counselor: Master's or doctoral degree in vocational counseling.

Assists students and others in selecting and training for a career. Does vocational testing and counseling. Specializes in occupational information. Serves on staff of schools and colleges; some in private practice.

Welfare Worker: Social work training.

Administers welfare funds; counsels and assists families on relief. On staff of city and state welfare departments.

YMCA—YWCA Worker: Training varies. Certification indicates a minimum of 30 graduate hours including counseling, religion, and group work.

On staff of YMCA and YWCA.

Appendix F. Bibliography

Church and Pastoral Care
Books

Clinebell, Howard J. *Basic Types of Pastoral Counseling.* Nashbille: Abingdon Press, 1966. (Contains a small section on pastoral counseling with the disadvantaged.)

―――――, ed. *Community Mental Health: The Role of Church and Temple.* Nashville: Abingdon Press, 1970. (Includes a chapter on "Pastoral Care of the Poor" by Don Browning.)

Huggins, Nathan I. *Protestants Against Poverty: Boston's Charities.* Westport, Conn.: Greenwood Publishing Co., 1971. (A historical account of the church and its reaction to poverty in one community.)

Jorns, Auguste. *The Quakers as Pioneers in Social Work.* New York: The Macmillan Co., 1931. (A historical account of one denomination and its attempt to provide poor relief.)

Keith-Lucas, Alan. *The Church and Social Welfare.* Philadelphia: The Westminster Press, 1962. (Brief and dated but suggestive.)

Kenrick, Bruce. *Come Out the Wilderness.* New York: Harper & Row, 1962. (A discussion of the East Harlem Protestant Parish.)

Miller, Haskell M. *Compassion and Community: An Appraisal of the Church's Changing Role in Social Welfare.* New York: Association Press, 1961. (Dated but comprehensive.)

Myers, Chauncie Kilmer. *Light the Dark Streets.* Garden City: Doubleday & Co., 1957. (The experiences of a minister in New York slums.)

Oates, Wayne E. *Pastoral Counseling in Social Problems.* Philadelphia: The Westminster Press, 1966.

Pastoral Services Through the Comprehensive Community Mental Health Center Program. South Carolina Department of Mental Health. Columbia, S.C., 1968.

Seifert, Harvey, and Clinebell, Howard. *Growth and Social Change.* Philadelphia: The Westminster Press, 1969.

Westberg, Granger E., and Draper, E. *Community Psychiatry and the Clergyman.* Springfield, Ill.: C. C. Thomas, 1966.

Articles

Bonthius, Robert H. "Pastoral Care for Structures—as Well as Persons." *Pastoral Psychology* 18 (May, 1967), 10.

———. "A Theology of Poverty: Prelude to Pastoral Care of the Poor." *Pastoral Psychology* 20 (November, 1969), 21-29.

Browning, Don. "The Challenge of the Poor." *Pastoral Psychology* 19 (March, 1968), 5-6.

———. "Pastoral Care and Social Ethics." *Pastoral Psychology* 20 (November, 1969), 5-6.

———. "Religion, Revelation, and the Strengths of the Poor." *Pastoral Psychology* 19 (March, 1968), 37-49.

Charland, William A., Jr. "Pastoral Counseling in the Context of Social Action." *Pastoral Psychology* 21 (October, 1970), 45-58.

Clinebell, Howard, J. and Seifert, Harvey. "Interdependence of the Pastoral and the Prophetic." *Pastoral Psychology* 20 (November, 1969), 7-14.

Coles, Robert. "God and the Rural Poor." *Psychology Today* (January, 1972), 33-40.

Collier, Robert M. "Contracts and Covenants: A Model for Interracial Social Action." *Pastoral Psychology* 21 (May, 1970), 39-48.

Harris, James R., M.D. "Poverty, Mental Health, and the Church." *Pastoral Psychology,* 20 (November, 1969), 45-48.

Oates, Wayne. "The Ethics of Poverty." *Pastoral Psychology* 20 (November, 1969), 30-44.

Pattison, E. Mansell. "Functions of the Clergy in Community Mental Health Centers." *Pastoral Psychology* 16 (May, 1965), 21-26.

Riessman, Frank. "Role-Playing and the Lower Socio-Economic Group." *Pastoral Psychology* 19 (March, 1968), 50-60.

Rylaarsdam, Coert. "Poverty and the Poor in the Bible." *Pastoral Psychology* 19 (March, 1968), 13-24.

Stinnette, Charles R., Jr. "Poverty—and Ministry as an Agency of Change." *Pastoral Psychology* 19 (March, 1968), 7-12.

Temple, Palmer C. "Training Values in Community Ministry." *Journal of Pastoral Care* 25 (June, 1971), 121-24.

Van Ness, Paul, and Van Ness, Elizabeth. "An Experimental Church-Related Counseling Program for the Inner City." *Pastoral Psychology* 20 (November, 1969), 15-20.

Way, Peggy. "Community Organization and Pastoral Care: Drum Beat For Dialogue." *Pastoral Psychology* 19 (March, 1968), 25-36.

Other Professional Literature

The following list is incomplete. We have attempted to include the basic books that one must frequently refer to. We started to accumulate a list of articles in the various professional journals, but that proved to be too extensive. The reader is referred to the *Reader's Guide to Periodicals*. Some of the most valuable material is found in journals.

Allen, Vernon L., ed. *Psychological Factors in Poverty*. Chicago: Markham Publishing Co., 1970.

Bagdikian, Ben H. *In the Midst of Plenty*. New York: New American Library, 1964. (Popularly written but useful.)

Bakke, E. Wight. *Citizens Without Work*. New Haven: Yale University Press, 1940.

Bremner, Robert H. *From the Depths: The Discovery of Poverty in the United States*. New York: New York University Press, 1956.

Brown, Claude. *Manchild in the Promised Land*. New York: The Macmillan Co., 1965.

Caplan, Gerald. *An Approach to Community Mental Health and Consultation*. Washington: U.S. Department of Health, Education and Welfare, 1961.

Caplovitz, David. *The Poor Pay More*. New York: The Free Press, 1963.

Conference on Economic Progress. *Poverty and Deprivation in the United States*. Washington, D.C.: Conference on Economic Progress, 1962.

Davis, Kenneth, ed. *Paradox of Poverty in America*. Bronx: H. W. Wilson Co., 1969.

Dollard, John, et al. *Frustration and Aggression*. New Haven: Yale University Press, 1939.

Duhl, Leonard J., ed. *The Urban Condition*. New York: Basic Books, 1963.

Dunne, George H. *Poverty in Plenty*. New York: P. J. Kenedy & Sons, 1964.

Elman, Richard. *The Poorhouse State: The American Way of Life on Public Assistance*. New York: Pantheon Books, 1966.

Galbraith, John Kenneth. *The Affluent Society*. New York: Mentor Books, 1958.

Gittings, James A. *Life Without Living: People of the Inner City*. Philadelphia: The Westminster Press, 1966.

Harrington, Michael. *The Other America: Poverty in the United States*. Baltimore: Penguin Books, 1962. (One of the most influential publications in the field.)

Henry, Jules. *Culture Against Man*. New York: Random House, 1963.

Hollingshead, A. B., and Redlich, F. C. *Social Class and Mental Illness*. New York: John Wiley & Sons, 1968.

Humphrey, Hubert H. *War On Poverty*. New York: McGraw-Hill Book Co., 1964.

Hunter, David R. *The Slums: Challenge and Response*. New York: The Free Press, 1964.

Harvey, Rodger. *Poverty and Mental Retardation*. New York: Random House, 1960.

Irelan, L. M., ed. *Low-Income Life Styles*. Washington, D.C.: United States Department of Health, Education and Welfare, Publication No. 14, 1966.

Kolko, Gabriel. *Wealth and Power in America*. New York: Praeger Publishers, 1962.

Langner, T. S., and Michael, S. T. *Life Stress and Mental Health*. New York: The Free Press, 1963.

Leinwand, Gerald, ed. *Poverty and the Poor*. New York: Washington Square Press, 1968.

Lewis, O. *La Vida: A Puerto Rican Family in the Culture of Poverty—San Juan and New York*. New York: Random House, 1966.

Lurie, Harry L., ed. *Encyclopedia of Social Work*. New York: National Association of Social Workers, 1965. (This is the most thorough and complete source of information available.)

McKinley, Donald. *Social Class and Family Life*. New York: The Free Press, 1964.

May, Edgar. *The Wasted Americans*. New York: Harper & Row, 1964.

Merton, Robert K. *Social Theory and Social Structure*. New York: The Free Press, 1957.

Miller, Herman P. *Rich Man, Poor Man.* New York: Thomas Y. Crowell Company, 1964.

Minuchin, Salvador, et al. *Families of the Slums, An Exploration of Their Structure and Treatment.* New York: Basic Books, 1967.

Morgan, James N., Martin H. David, Wilbur J. Cohen, and Harvey E. Brazer. *Income and Welfare in the United States.* New York: McGraw-Hill Book Co., 1962.

Myers, Jrome K., and Bean, Lee L. *A Decade Later: A Follow Up of Social Class and Mental Illness.* New York: John Wiley & Sons, 1968.

Myrdal, Gunnar. *Challenge to Affluence.* New York: Random House, 1963.

Pearl, Arthur, and Riessman, Frank. *New Careers for the Poor.* New York: The Free Press, 1965.

President's Appalachian Regional Commission. *Appalachia.* Washington, D.C.: U.S. Government Printing Office, 1964.

Redl, Fritz, and Wineman, David. *Children Who Hate.* New York: The Free Press, 1951.

Riessman, Frank. *The Culturally Deprived Child.* New York: Harper & Row, 1962.

————, Cohen, Jerome, and Pearl, Arthur. *Mental Health of the Poor.* New York: The Free Press, 1964.

Shostak, Arthur B., and Gomberg, William. *New Perspectives on Poverty.* Englewood Cliffs, N.J.: Prentice-Hall, 1965.

————. *Blue-Collar World: Studies of the American Worker.* Englewood Cliffs, N.J.: Prentice-Hall, 1964.

Simon, Arthur. *Faces of Poverty.* New York: The Macmillan Co., 1968.

Stern, Philip and De Vincent, George. *Shame of a Nation.* New York: Astor-Honor Inc., 1965.

Steward, Maxwell. *The Poor Among Us—Challenge and Opportunity.* New York: Public Affairs Pamphlet Company, 1967.

Stone, Robert C. *Family Life Styles Below the Poverty Line.* Lexington, Mass.: Heath, 1966.

Titmuss, Richard T. *Essays on the Welfare State.* New Haven: Yale University Press, 1958.

Williams, Frederick, ed. *Language and Poverty.* Chicago: Markham, 1971.